I0616387

YOU ARE MY WHOLE EARTH

A Daddy's Love For His Sons

AARON RYAN

AWARD-WINNING AUTHOR OF THE BESTSELLING
ALIEN INVASION SAGA **DISSONANCE**, THE CHRISTIAN
DYSTOPIAN SAGA **THE END, FORECAST, THE SLIDE,
THE PHOENIX EXPERIMENT, YOU'RE GOING
STRAIGHT TO HELEN (IN A HANDBASKET), GOD IS
NOT SANTA,** AND MANY MORE

Published in 2025, Edition 1.

eBook ISBN: 978-1-965372-60-9
Paperback ISBN: 978-1-965372-61-6
Hardcover ISBN: 978-1-965372-62-3

Edited by CM LLC. Published independently.

Cover art by CM LLC.

This is a work of nonfiction. Any similarities to
persons living or dead, or actual events is purely
coincidental.

For Sweeps, Bren & AJ:
my true loves.

Thank you for being my whole Earth.

Chapters

"My father gave me the greatest gift anyone could give another person: he believed in me."

- Jim Valvano

"The power of a dad in a child's life is unmatched."

- Justin Ricklefs

"A father doesn't tell you that he loves you. He shows you."

- Dimitri The Stoneheart

Note on A.I.

We live in an age of AI. Every day, more and more services spring up promising revolutionary and innovative results using artificial intelligence. The authoring industry is not immune to this.

I want every one of my readers to know that not once did I employ, nor will I *ever* employ, the use of AI to sculpt any part of any of my stories. Those who know me know that I am staunchly and adamantly opposed to such cheats.

I'm very proud to be a verified human. The ability to create is a gift that I was endowed by my Creator, and I will never forfeit that nor set it aside to propagate something synthetic and imitative.

Everything you've read by me in this book, and in my other works, is 100% entirely created by me, the genuine article. I'm a verified human, and always will be.

To my fellow authors, I urge you to preserve the sacred gift of human creation and never stoop to such lows. Always cherish this gift you've been given. If you encounter writer's block, take a break. Don't cop out. Don't take the road more traveled by. Don't cheat. Toe the line for all of us, and keep creation – *true* unadulterated creation – alive.

Long live humanity.

Also, if you're an author – or even a budding one – I'd love to personally extend an invite to you to join me in two unique groups on Facebook: the *Authors & Writers ONLY* group of which I am the admin, and my own personal group, the *Author Aaron Ryan Group*. The first group is one where you can connect with thousands of other authors across the globe, ask questions, learn and grow as a writer, and network. Grapes grow best in bunches, after all. The second is my own personal group. I find much higher engagement in my *group* than with my Facebook *page*.

I also welcome other authors to join me there for free giveaways, news, and also to learn why I self-publish, what benefits there are in being a writer-entrepreneur, and more. As a fellow author, I'm always here to help you in any way I can.

God bless you as you use the gift of creation to sculpt
your stories and books. May they, and you, be
utterly successful.

Sincerely,
Aaron Ryan,

Verified Human

Chapter 1: Utter Craziness

Being a parent doesn't come with a set of instructions. There's no roadmap or Thomas Guide. There's no one-size-fits all. It's hysteria to the power of insanity multiplied by frenzy, with a dash of tempest and a full helping of helplessness.

My boys are unique. They are (currently, though this increases in number seemingly by the *minute*, leaving me to wonder where all the time went) 9 and 6 years old, and they are the best and worst of me. They are all kinds of rambunctious, steroidal shrieking adrenaline-filled energy beasts, sapping our aging vigor right out of us as we struggle to keep up, panting with everything that is in us. They push our buttons, they demand, they petition, and they do all three both with and without manners. I have seen traits in each one of them that leave me speechless, as if God saw fit to take my formula, hit CTRL-C, and then hit CTRL-V on some template somewhere, sprinkle in a few extra deviating lines of code, and out pops this brand new lifeform that looks kind of like me, talks kind of like me, walks kind of like me, yet is utterly different from me.

Each of my sons are completely unique in every way, and that's the formula that they were given; the DNA they were prescribed; the computer code they were programmed with.

Brennan is our right-brain creative, and Asher is our left-brain intellect. This is something you cannot plan. They are utterly diametrically opposed to each other and yet fully complement each other in ways we could not have anticipated whatsoever.

I'll talk about each son in separate chapters, but for now, suffice it to say that they require constant involvement and investment…. and it's incumbent upon me to give both.

Involvement, because they are my sons, and I want them to know how utterly important they are to me. I want them to know that I appraise their value higher than my smartphone. Higher than my own book I'd like to read. Higher than my own 'me time' that I had carefully carved out of our schedule for that unbusied Saturday morning that I was, you know, kind of really looking forward to but now must put the kibosh on because Brennan REAAAAAAAAAALLY needs to show me this craft he made of all the variations of creatures from *Godzilla x Kong: The New Empire.* Or because Asher REEEEEEEEAAAAAAAALLLLLLY wants me to behold him complete the entire game of Super Mario World and isn't this move cool where I thrash Bowser, Dad?

Yes, son, it's *very* cool.

Every day is relatively the same:

- Wake up.
- Get ready for school.
- Come home.
- Do chores.
- Go to ninja training or piano lessons.
- Have dinner.
- iPad time. Or game console time.
- Bath time.

- Play.
- Stories.
- Prayer. (We always end on prayer, which I highly recommend. Let prayer be the key of the morning and the bolt of the evening!)
- And then bedtime.

Some days vary, but most follow this unique and trusted routine. But *all* are filled with craziness between those bullet points.

Now, I know, as parents, my wife and I follow a very carefully constructed formula: a skillset of responses that allow us to commend our children for something they've said or seen or heard or done, and we're commending them without even having laid eyes or ears on what they've said or seen or heard or done. I do not know where this skillset comes from other than pure magic, because I took no classes. All I know is that whenever I'm deeply engrossed in whatever I'm doing, if my sons come up to me and start droning on about something important to them, I am deftly able to brandish sudden responses such as "That's amazing." "Wow, that's so cool, I've never seen *anything* so cool!" "Uh-huh, that's great honey!"

tightens wrench on bolt under sink without even glancing at whatever my son is displaying

I'm pretty aware that every parent comes with this superhuman ability to creatively outsource our attentiveness for the moment, simply affirming our children because we have to simply affirm our children. There isn't a Plan B. There isn't another option.

We *must* affirm our children. We *must* communicate to them how utterly important they are and how utterly fascinating we think everything that *they* think is fascinating... is. We don't have a choice. We grown men and women were endowed this superpower by a very calculated DNA process with a controlled release that happens to kick in, oh, right about the time our children start developing the ability of show and tell. I can't explain it, so don't ask. All I know is that they want to show me everything, and I don't have that kind of time. So I end up either *making* time, or pretending that the time they just took to show me what was so important to them *is* important.

All too often, I've erred on the latter, when I should
have embraced the former. My kids *love* showing me
things, telling me things, sharing things. In their little
world, the things that are they are experiencing, they
are doing so for perhaps the very first time. It's new
and exciting to them! Their eyes light up. They want
me to experience what they're experiencing. They
want to tell me all about it. And it's incumbent upon
me as a parent to stop and listen to my boys.

It can get crazy sometimes, sure. There will be times
where I really *have* to get all us all in the car for
church. They will be late for school so they *must* get
their coat and backpack on *NOW*. We're way past
bedtime so they *can't* stand there and tell me all about
how cool Mothra is. (She's actually wicked cool; I
suggest checking her out post-haste.) Sometimes,
time really *is* of the essence, and whatever they want
to sow into my day must wait.

But I can always make it up to them. I can always
demonstrate the utmost of attentiveness to them
every chance I get. Do I always? Certainly not: I'm a
human and also a complete idiot. But I must try. I
always *must... try... my... hardest.* Even when they
fry every last chip and try every last nerve in my

body. Their constant questions. *Lawd.* I remember seeing a meme one time that said, "Once I became a parent I finally understood the scene where Yoda gets so tired of answering Luke's questions that he just dies." This now makes absolute sense to me.

It can definitely get crazy. Parsing through all of that hysteria, however, I have two beautiful tiny humans growing up in my home in desperate need of love, affirmation, attention, and guidance. Little do they know that the Daddy they've been given is just about as crazy as his offspring, so I'm on the right wavelength with them. My wife, Janine, the boys' Mama, is much more like Asher in that she's a left brain intellect. She's less zany and far more grounded than me. (I do make every effort to wave to her from fifty-thousand feet up.) She keeps the boys' feet on the ground in ways I will never be able to.

I keep their heads in the clouds. Where it's crazy.

Most people who know me know that I have a penchant for wearing funny T-Shirts. One of my all-time favorites is the word 'Fatherhood' sprawled out in Jurassic Park letters, positioned above a T-Rex, and

below that, the words 'Like a Walk In The Park.'
Fatherhood truly *is* a walk in the park.... *Jurassic*
Park, that is! It's got its share of scares, frights, and
bumps... ...and I wouldn't trade it for the world. It's
the adventure that brings balance, and we all need it.
Especially us Dads.

Speaking of Dads, my favorite day of the year is
Father's Day. Not Christmas, not my birthday, not
the 4th of July. Father's Day. It's the day I feel most
loved. Perhaps its because of the two little reasons
that my wife and I worked so hard for. Perhaps it's
because it conveys upon me a tremendous sense of
purpose and worth. Perhaps it's because I get to be
honored for being someone's Daddy.

Or, perhaps it's all three in one. I *love* being a Daddy,
and I love being celebrated for a day where I get to
celebrate the three reasons for me being a daddy...
right back. My wife, my firstborn, and my baby. It is
my favorite day of the year, bar none.

Now that you have a rough idea of how I feel about
fatherhood and life, let me introduce you to my life's
two greatest little accomplishments.

DEAR BRENNAN AND ASHER:

You are my whole Earth. You are my reason for living. You are my pride and joy. You are my life's greatest achievements.

I love you with all my heart and am immeasurably proud of both of you. I love how crazy you make our lives together, and, for a guy who has always prided himself on organization and keeping things in their place, thank you for the hysteria that you bring that upsets the natural order and causes me to roll with the punches; to adapt. In short, thank you for all the messes that require me to work on my patience. Thank you for the frenzy that forces me to employ skills I didn't know I had. As the old adage goes, *adapt or die*. Thank you for literally saving my life by forcing me to adapt. Thank you for forcing me into positions of flexibility so that I can see that life is about more than just structure and order.

It's about soaking up every ounce of silliness in every single moment that I can.

Love,
Daddy

Chapter 2: Brennan

Friday, June 19th 2015 is a day I will never forget.

I had just brought our two-year-old Lab/Chow/Shar Pei back in from going morning potty, and it was early. I was downstairs in my bathrobe, and my wife of three years was upstairs in the master bathroom in our little Shoreline home. I casually walked around the downstairs, turning things on, giving everything a once-over and appraising the comforts of our little home, and then I came to rest at the bottom of the stairs, gazing up at her.

"Honey?" she asked. "Huh?" I replied. "Come here," she stated curiously.

I couldn't see exactly what she was doing, but her tone intrigued me. I headed up the stairs, every wooden step of the 1958 house creaking under my weight. Before I got to the bathroom, I saw what she was holding, and, more than that, I saw the expression on her face.

The next thing out of my mouth was "That's *pregnant!* That's *pregnant,* honey!" She dithered, unsure if it really meant what it said, at which point I tried to assert that I had seen so many pregnancy tests displayed in the *Glow* app we had been using, and many of them were exactly the same. Before I could complete my excited assertion, she melted into an optimistic – and nervous – smile, accepting the precious gravity of our new reality, and sunk into my embrace. And I into hers! We both just laughed, deep-throated and full of joy, together. Actually, it was cry-laughing, as ugly as that can get, still reverberating with utter joy.

We had tried *so* hard. Those very stairs I just came up? Yep, they're the same stairs I collapsed upon one morning after sending her off to work, my emotions so racked with pain and sadness that we *still* hadn't conceived yet. I fell upon those stairs and bawled, not even making it up to our bedroom. We wanted to be parents *so* bad, we could feel it in our teeth.

The hard part was that we weren't getting any younger. In 2015, I was already 42, and she was 39. We found each other later in life, we got married later in life, and we were trying to conceive… later in life. The odds were against us, but we pressed on.

Well, Janine went on to take another pregnancy test later that day in the bathroom stall at work, and sent me a glowing photo of her in the stall, *so* excited, so radiant, so consumed by joy, and there, clearly for all our eyes to see, just as there was early that morning, were *two lines.*

*We were **finally** pregnant.*

Janine did everything right, including not getting offended when the gynecologist's office labeled her 'Advanced Maternal Age.' At one point clinics were actually using the term *geriatric,* but I think due to offended and hormonal pregnant women not liking that term and possibly having access to weapons, they wisely chose to adapt the moniker to something less inciting.

Fast-forward to February 12th 2016, and our little guy arrived, with all ten digits, a healthy conical alien head *full* of jet black hair, and curious eyes that beheld the world full of wonder. Janine and I both had colds at the time, and he was born into that, so the first few weeks of his life were spent hiccupping, sneezing, and coughing. Poor little guy! In fact, the first night after he was born, I was staying with my wife and sleeping on the, ahem, *uber*-comfortable window bench, when Brennan decided to display an incurable case of the hiccups. I freaked out and ran out to the nurses' station, practically wailing, "Uh, help! What do we do? Our son has hiccups!" I made sure to gesture frantically.

Both nurses just stared at me blankly. One of them actually asked, "Yes? And?" To which I replied coolly, "Oh, well, *clears throat* uh, nothing. I, uh, ya know, just *cough cough* just wanted you to know. It's cool." Followed by my walking back to our hospital room in embarrassment. Lesson? *They're hiccups, dude. Chill.*

Brennan clocked in at 6.8 pounds, measuring 20," born at 3:54pm in the afternoon. We bawled, sneezed, coughed, and loved all over him. It was beautiful. And... kind of gross.

Fast forward to today. He's an amazing child, incredibly creative, a *huge* button pusher, overly dramatic, crazily introspective, easily moody, and one heckuva insanely cool kid. The 3D crafts that this boy puts together, I *swear* he's going to get employed at the Stan Winston School of Special FX and make a lot of money someday. And I want some of it.

But before that? Brennan was born during a time of great trauma for Janine and I. We were currently being cyberstalked by an individual in Arizona who was relentless, and was threatening to sue us and other people. We didn't want to go to court (who does?); we wanted to just celebrate our new baby. But we were in hiding from this man so that he couldn't serve us court summons. Consequently, we were living in the back of our house, with the shades drawn and the lights off. We were living in fear and anxiety.

Additionally, Janine struggled with milk production at the time, which was highly emotionally taxing for her. We were securing frozen donated milk from others – *God bless the communities that exist to facilitate this!* – and didn't want Brennan to be on formula all the time. My poor beautiful wife just wanted to nurse her son, but he was failing to latch, and early on had even approached 'failure to thrive.' We were first-time parents; we didn't know a lot. We tried, just like the rest of brand new parents out there, to just do our best and to take care of him. Eventually, he turned out fine, and he was truly a looker as an infant, as well as a toddler, and is an incredibly handsome kid. One day, we tell him, the girls will be *throwing* themselves at him. To which our 9-year-old replies, with a stiff upper lip, "Yeah, and I'm gonna run in the opposite direction!" This kid looks away and groans anytime someone kisses someone in a movie. That'll change soon.

But, what do you think happened to Brennan through all of that anxiety that we were living in? Our firstborn became one very anxious little boy. Babies can feel that tension. They can tell when something's off with you, and Brennan, being the little sponge that babies are, soaked up that tension. As a result, he struggled with bedwetting for years, is easily offended, nervous, anxious, and can be moody. It's amazing how all of that went into him.

Do I resent what we went through that formed parts of Brennan's disposition and personality? Not at all. Not one bit. He is precisely who God created him to be, and no one pulls the wool over God's eyes. (He made sheep; I'm sure he can handle seeing through their wool.) Brennan is *precisely* who he is supposed to be. Does he have flares of anxiety? Yes. Does he still wet the bed occasionally? Yes. Does he whine and complain? Yes. Does he make a big scene when he has to go out to the garage for something but doesn't want to go alone? Yes. (See: *all the time.*) Would I have it any other way? *Fuggedaboudit.*

I remember a time when I was clipping tiny little Brennan's fingernails with that miniscule surgical nail clipper you get from Walgreen's that should come with an overly large warning that says something to the effect of:

CAUTION: USE OF THIS PRODUCT MAY IN FACT RESULT IN THE INADVERTENT SNIPPING OFF OF YOUR BABY'S FLESH, CAUSING THEM TO CRY HORRENDOUS CROCODILE TEARS WHICH WILL MAKE YOU QUESTION YOUR SELF-WORTH AND COMPEL YOU TO ADOPT TITLES SUCH AS

'WORST PARENT IN THE SOLAR SYSTEM EVER,'
BEFORE YOU SURRENDER TO THE KNOWLEDGE
THAT YOU UTTERLY SUCK AND ARE THEN
ENCASED IN LAVA AND LAUNCHED INTO THE
DEPTHS OF SPACE.

I've been there, believe me. I had done this, and oh boy, did Brennan let me have it. He was only a month or so old, but I accidentally pinched him with the nail clipper, and had actually drawn a bit of blood! My eyes flew to his face in a panic, and I can still see, as in slow motion, his little face scrunch together in agony, preceding a soul-wrenching and never-ending shriek that rent the heavens. It was *awful*. I took that little infant and pressed his howling mouth to my ear, and just whispered the following to him:

Let me have it. I deserve it. I can take it.

I let him howl and howl and howl (after I had staunched the minor flow of blood on his finger) right into my ear, and I absorbed all of his pint-sized wrath, letting him vent his sadness and consternation right into me. I needed to. Why?

Because he needed to be heard. I love my son, and I want him to be heard. I want him to know that his feelings are valid, legitimate, and important. What I did, though a complete accident, hurt him, and oh boy did he let me know. (As a baby, anytime Brennan would be in a crying fit with Janine, she would say theatrically to him, "I know! You just tell me all about it!" Adorable.) I needed to absorb that pain, and to receive what he had to say. That awful, tragic moment, and my decision to take responsibility through it and feel what he was feeling, made me a better Daddy, I believe.

I'll never forget the "Twinkle Twinkle" version by *Baby Sleep Through The Night · Lullabies for Babies and Children' Songs.* I… LOVE… THAT… SONG. There were so many nights where I would put Brennan to bed and then I would rest in the big, plush Safari chair in his room, listening to various instrumental kids' songs cycle through a playlist. Whenever that song would come on, I would drop everything I was doing, turn my phone over, turn my palms up, and just *receive.* The song *so* moved me. It's like a combination of harp and guitar strings, and it's so glorious in its simplicity. I've never heard anything calmer. So many nights with my son five feet from me in his crib while I sat there in the dark just receiving. He was the most beautiful thing I had ever seen already, and was now enveloped and wrapped in the beauty of this song nearly every night. It moved me to tears. It still does to this day.

As Brennan grew up, my wife and I could instantly see his affinity for artistic pursuits, his musical bent, his skill in identifying (and singing back to us) various songs, and other right-brain talent. It has been such a wonder to behold.

Brennan is my carbon copy, my tiny mirror, my junior doppelganger. He is the very best of me: creativity, sensitivity, manners, drive, passion, and the very worst of me: impulsivity, brooding, moodiness, whining. He is *just* like me. This helps me as his Daddy to be more aware of who he is, how he is, and where he's at. I can see plenty similarities between how he responds to things in life and how I myself respond. This equips me to help walk him through it.

On the other hand, I come from a background of tough love, stemming from my grandmother, and boy does that ever work to undermine me. "Suck it

up," "Stop your crying," "Tough it out," "Be a man,"
and other admonitions don't really do anything to
help Brennan be *heard*. I constantly find myself
barking those commands as my first order of business
rather than getting down to his level and letting him
be heard, and it's a battle that I've lost many, many
times with him. Barking at him is erring on the side
of steering him back to strength (which there is
nothing inherently wrong with), whereas letting him
feel heard is erring on the side of grace. Empathizing
with him is part of the latter, and Brennan
desperately needs empathy in order to feel heard.
He's that type of child. It is something I constantly
work on.

All in all, we have a dynamo in this kid, who is
incredibly well-mannered (and complimented
frequently on it), reads like a champ, runs full-tilt
with a frenzy, spins and cavorts like a whirling
dervish, and creates 3D crafts like a demigod. He is a
barrel of energy, a Pandora's Box of frenzy, he is
competitive to a 50,000-mile-high fault, and I
wouldn't have him any other way. I love my
firstborn; he made me a daddy, after all, and I owe
him forever for that.

He's not a sports nut or an athlete; that's not his makeup (we have to beat him with a stick to get him outside.) He's not a debater or a scholar-in-the-making; that's also not his makeup (he's still shy about being up in front of people). He is a creator, just like his Daddy. And if there's one thing that I love, I *love* creating. As an author, and, in fact, with so many of my careers, that's what I've been privileged to do: create. Brennan is following closely in my footsteps. I predict he'll be an artist, an artisan, a poet, a singer, a musician, a raw talent blessed with so many performative gifts. That's just who he is... and I love who he is, and who he's becoming.

We've laughed together crazily, we've wrestled and tickled each other until we've cried, we've competed in slap fights, we've bested each other, we've hurt each other's feelings inadvertently, and we've lain in peace together, calmly restoring the balance and resting in the reminder that we are both loved.

This little boy is, after all, a little boy. He doesn't need to be treated like he knows everything, because he doesn't. He doesn't need to think I expect perfection out of him, because I don't. He needs to be allowed to be just that: a little boy, growing, learning, messing up, learning some more, fixing things, improving, amassing knowledge as he goes, trying, failing, trying, succeeding, giving and receiving grace, assimilating knowledge with practical application, witnessing, processing, figuring things out, exploring, growing, and, again… learning.

I LOVE watching him learn.

TO BRENNAN:

I love you, Brennan. You are my beloved son, in whom I am well pleased. I am inordinately proud of you. I watch you and wonder what kind of man you'll become, nervous as all heck but confident that you're going to take on this whole world and conquer. I love who you are, what you are, why you are, and how you are. Everything about you is utterly amazing, and you are filled with an awe for this world, as well as incredible talent that blows me away and takes me by storm. I am proud of you, *proud* of you, proud of *you*, my beloved son, and I can never say that enough.

I am enamored with how you are developing, who you are becoming, how you understand humor, how

everything is a wonder to you, how you can take the
most minute ingredients and fashion some physically
mind-boggling and stellar craft out of it, and you do
that time and time again. What you are able to
conjure up out of the imaginary recesses of your
mind blows us away multiple times a day. Yes, our
paper, tape, and pen budget is through the freaking
roof, but we LOVE you for it. I just wish I had
somewhere large enough to contain all your crafts.
Note to self: buy a massive storage shed.

Anyway, Bren, I love being your daddy. I love the
rich privilege that it is. You complete me, Bub, and
I'm so proud to call you mine.

You are my whole Earth, and everything in it.

Love,
Daddy

Chapter 3: Asher

Many friends of ours who are also parents share a similar story. They recounted how they tried and tried to have their first child, and then they finally did. Following that, they felt like they simply blinked and sneezed - *BAM!* And then there were two.

That is – *totally* – our story. Granted, it happened three-point-five years later, but I will freely admit that it took Janine and I three hundred and seventy nine attempts to conceive Brennan. For those who are not sure what fresh craziness they just read, *yes, we counted.*

We were actually advised to count by our former pastor and friend, Bill. Bill and his wife used to keep a yearly jar of M&Ms. Their goal was to try to outdo themselves from the year prior, where, each time they were intimate, they would put an M&M in the jar for that year. The next year, each time they had sex, they would take an M&M out of the previous year's jar and transfer it to the new jar. If they ran out of M&M's, then that meant that they had beat the previous year's record. Then, for each time they came together, they would simply add an M&M from a new bag into the current jar.

Well, Janine and I desperately wanted a child, if you recall, and we were most definitely keeping count. It took us 379 times to conceive Brennan. Well, then it took us like *five* times to conceive Asher. So weird. And then our housemaid came along and ate our sex (read: M&M's), which was both hilarious *and* thoroughly disgusting. We subsequently lost count and figured, well, that's that. But we got a baby out of it, so… *Bonus!*

The odd thing is that both times, we were utterly *convinced* that we would have a girl. We were even prophesied over by different people – who don't even know each other – that they saw a vision of my wife Janine "running through a field with a little girl." All three of these people had the same exact vision, so, here we go, we get pregnant with Brennan, and naturally assume, *yay! Here's our daughter!*

Nope. We were perplexed... but not disappointed. A son is awesome news! And we were just so elated to have conceived, it could have been a walrus and we would still have been tickled, although aquariums are difficult to install in one's home.

But then, sure enough, we blinked and we sneezed and we got pregnant again. Both of us looked at each other and said, "Aha! OK, got it. *Now* here's our daughter." We just knew that *this* time we'd have a girl, like the prophesies of old foretold.

Nope.

Prophesies suck. We were seriously confused. I'll never forget the baffled look on my wife's face when she got the blood work results on a printout from the gynecologist at a regular appointment, and it clearly indicated "BOY." Again, she was not disappointed – neither of us were – we were just thoroughly confused. What were these prophesies? Who was this little girl these three unrelated people had seen 'running with Janine through a field'?

The prophets must be drunk, we concluded. Either that, or it had some hidden meaning, *a la* Janine making peace with her childhood self or some psycho-babble like that, and it was grown-up Janine running hand-in-hand with little-girl-Janine. Or… something. The vote is still out. Please hold for the results on your prophecy. Your call is very important to us.

All that to say that we had Asher on June 12th, 2019, and it was… nothing short of excruciating. Whereas our first pregnancy went off without a hitch, Asher was developing all kinds of size issues in utero, gestational diabetes, and it was like he was drinking all the fluid in there and would run out before it was time to give birth. Therefore, we had to induce him. And let me just say, it was… horrendous. I've written about this before in an earlier voiceover blog about how traumatizing Asher's birth was for the both of us, and I thought, rather than reinvent the wheel, I'm going to just insert this here for you to experience what we did. Keep in mind this was written in 2019, so some of the references might sound a bit dated. Anyway, here goes:

===

One In The Oven

It was the morning of October 25th, 2018. My son Brennan and I were in the living room, playing. Nothing too out of the ordinary, except I had neglected to check the toaster setting for my English Muffins, which would soon be blackened bricks.

I knew my wife was upstairs in the shower, and I also knew that today was a great day. She and I had both just come back from a marriage retreat two weeks prior that was *much needed*. Holy cow did we need that. It was a very difficult year, with lots of stress and some fighting. OK actually it was a little bit of stress, and lots of fighting. Don't need to pinpoint the reasons why at this stage, just suffice it to say that we desperately needed the retreat. We had left Brennan with MeeMaw and Pop-Pop and headed off to a hotel in Tacoma, where we stayed for the whole weekend. We were anxious to pick him up and see him again on our way home, but we really enjoyed the retreat and were able to patch up some wounds and hit a reset button of sorts.

That was two weeks ago.

This morning, I happened to be lounging on the loveseat wearing only my boxers, because yeah. It was just a loungy morning. I was scrolling through something on my phone, when my wife emerged from the stairs in a towel with her hair all bedraggled. I looked up and said "Hi, honey!" Without a word, she approached me, towel wrapped up to her neck and one of her hands on the inside of it, and the other on the outside. It didn't occur to me that she was holding something.

In her eloquent way, she began, "Listen, I just wanted to tell you that I know you've been working hard." *I had been.* "And I know you've been depressed about your weight lately." *Lately? More like my whole life, but please continue.* "And I just wanted to tell you that I love you, and I'm proud of you, and let's gain weight together."

She pulled it out, and I saw that glorious wand of pink and blue, with two distinct blue lines through the readout screen at the end. I instantly jumped up and shouted, "NO WAY!!!!" and burst into tears as I grabbed her and hugged her. Brennan glanced over at us, registered that something was happening that didn't equal the intensity and wonder of *The Incredibles 2*, and wrote us off straightaway.

We jumped, we laughed, we cried. We couldn't believe that we were pregnant again. We thought it would never happen. We're a bit older and we started a bit later. When Brennan came along, he was a surprise in his own right. To know that we would now be on our way to becoming a family of *four* was just downright beautiful and majestic. I remember picking Brennan up and twirling him around over and over and over and exclaiming "You're gonna be a big brother you're gonna be a big brother you're gonna be a big brother!!" He didn't know what brother meant yet – at least I don't think, but he knew what big was. Either way, his expression said, in no uncertain terms, *please put me back down so I can resume watching the Incredibles 2, which you're interrupting, thankyouverymuch.*

We couldn't believe it. We sat and talked for a while and just giggled. It was amazing. That was October 25th 2018.

It's Go Time.

Remember *Aliens*, directed by James Cameron in 1986? Yeah. Favorite movie of all time. The character *Hicks* says that to Ripley, and he means it, because it is. It's quite literally *go time*.

The same was true for us. We knew the day was close, but we also knew it could be *today*. Over the past few months my beautiful wife had been diagnosed with gestational diabetes, and so she had to watch her sugar intake, and actually had to puncture her beautiful fingers four times a day and test her levels. She had to drink her weight in water each day.

She had a checkup on Monday, June 10th 2019 at Evergreen Women's Clinic in Kirkland, and they had said that her fluid was a bit low. Moreover, if she didn't get her levels up by that coming Wednesday – two short days later – they would have to induce.

Janine had heard horror stories of induction. Being induced is basically – from my sheep-brained man's perspective, telling the body to be ready for birth when it actually isn't ready, and turning everything into a locomotive for delivery. She did not want that.

I don't blame her. My cousin just had his second son, and his wife had to be induced; she went from 5 to 10 in 45 minutes, and she had said that it was excruciating. I'd rather puke coat hangers based on the horror story I heard of it. Yikes.

Janine obeyed. She drank even more water, she walked regularly, she ate well, and her levels were always good. Be that as it may, when we went into the ultrasound room on Wednesday June 12th 2019 and the technician said her fluid was still looking kinda low, we knew what that meant. Janine's mouth creased into a frown, and her eyes closed. She wanted so badly to have this baby *naturally*. Brennan was born naturally, but she wanted our second son to be born naturally, and on time, too. Not early. Not by someone else's medicine, but by her own body saying it was time.

We verified it with the doctor, and she said that yes, Janine would have to be induced today. We were prepared, sure enough, as we had brought the diaper bag, Brennan's little bag of clothes and food and snacks and toys, and Janine's hospital bag. We had sent warning texts out to friends and family who were going to take care of our dog and who might need to be called upon, but still, it was begrudgingly so. That baby was coming today, and not by our own will.

I dropped Janine off at Evergreen Women's Clinic and then brought Brennan home to be watched by a longtime family friend who dearly loves him. She was elated to watch him until relief arrived in the form of my brother-in-law who would stay the night, and I would pick him back up from school the following morning. I scatterbrainedly (it's a word, promise) explained everything in detail about dog food, cat food, Brennan food, her food, the pool rules, changing, where diapers are, where the remote is, where the phone numbers are, where the toys are, where we'll be, where we *wanted* to be, etc. Then, yours truly was screaming back down the highway in the "good to go" lane. I didn't care about the fee; I needed to be with my wife.

When I found her in room 2141 (which, coincidentally was the *exact* same room at Evergreen Hospital that Asher's big brother had been born in 3.5 years earlier!), she was doing well and in good spirits. She was fine. It was a bummer, but it would be fine. She had already been administered some penicillin and Pitocin, and so we were underway. A little unprepared and incredulous, but willing and ready.

A Veritable Nightmare

What I'm about to describe can only be described as... indescribable. I still shake my head how anyone – ANYONE – can go through what I witnessed my wife go through. Even as I write this, the PTSD in me is kicking in, and I am tearing up remembering the utter pain and trauma we both experienced.

Janine began the slow labor climb at 3:30pm, and things were fine: she walked, she stretched, she talked with our doula, she rested, she ate. At 8:41pm, after some stretching by the doula's boss (she was more experienced and it was wonderful having her there!) I was behind Janine steadying her standing legs when I saw some droplets hit the floor. I was just reaching for a rag to mop them up, when I heard a splash, and then there was, um, *more* water. *Lots* more. Janine's water broke. No turning back now. Here we go.

It's go time.

Her contractions had slowly escalated, because that's what Pitocin does: it tells the body that it's in labor and essentially *forces* it into labor. The contractions were 2-4 minutes apart, then 2-3, then 2, and they were getting stronger. By 9pm, she was starting to hurt, and was moaning. I was behind her, praying for her, thinking in my sheep-brain that it would be just like last time.

It was nothing like last time.

By 9:45 she was in the tub, and she was hurting, really hurting. The last time we were in this room, it was a slow climb, but it was manageable, and she moaned very little, and pushed very controlled… and she owned all of it. Now, her body was taking off without her, and it was like she had a coat stuck in the door as the train was rolling down the tracks.

#Warrior

I use the hashtag because that's what I use in social media when I talk about her. She is a warrior, a freaking warrior made out of stern stuff. She's been through a lot in her life, as we all have, but ultimately, she's been through some *other* things that lots of people have not, and she's weathered them. I love my wife. She is made of untearable fabric, and unbeatable metal that has been forged in the fiery lava of volcanos. She's like the stuff that airplane black boxes are made out of, which they always seem to recover after a crash. (Which makes me wonder, if those black boxes are relatively indestructible, why don't they just make the whole airplane out of that stuff? Things that make you go *hmmm…*) Or she's like the One Ring from *The Lord of the Rings.* If the ring was in fact unbreakable, then she was what it was made out of. She is unbreakable, unbeatable, unmeltable. (I forbid you from chucking her into a volcano to test this theory.) I'll say it again: she is a freaking warrior. I'm so very proud of her.

But by 10pm, she was really, really hurting. As a husband of a wife in labor, there is absolutely nothing I can do. There are in fact things I should NOT do under any circumstances. I knew what those were. My job was to hold her hand, let her clutch me, cry against me, pull me, bite me. She needed someone of *equally* stern material to weather this storm with her. They couldn't find anyone, so they picked me.

Have you ever been disassembled? I have. It happened on June 12th, 2019.

Janine started screaming and convulsing. She was being ripped apart from the inside, almost like an alien chestburster was on its way out. Her body was forcing her to relinquish control, and she had to simply tag along and weather the pain. She screamed. She screamed more. And then she kept screaming. We got her out of the tub, and put her in bed, and I asked, confusedly, in hopes of helping her, "Where's the epidural? When can she get that?" The doula boss looked at me and said, "You don't understand; she's having a baby in the next five minutes."

What happened in the next five minutes I'll never really concretely be able to grasp. I heard my wife yell screams I didn't even know lungs and larynxes could manufacture. I heard terror and sadness and uncontrollable shrieks. She grabbed me and bit me and pulled my hair and my clothes. I desperately tried to console her, voicing words into her ears and reminding her that I'm here.

Me, the voiceover artist. I, who get hired and paid to encourage and motivate people, was stripped of all my power and ability, as I could simply do nothing except absorb her anguish. And when I say anguish, I mean absolute utter unbearable angina, suffering and torment.

My second son, Asher Justus, was born at 10:21pm on June 12th, 2019, at Evergreen Hospital, Kirkland, Washington... and I had no idea. For the first five minutes of his life I didn't even know he was there. All I could hear, reverberating in my ears and my heart and my soul, was the pain of my wife, and for the first time ever in my seven years of marriage, I thought I was going to lose my wife right through my fingers. I couldn't understand why it was *that* painful – I mean painful? Sure. But *that* painful, like *it-sounded-like-she-was-being-sawed-in-two* painful? I had no idea my son had even been born, I was *so* preoccupied with not losing my wife.

My son had come out, and my wife was still screaming for a bit, but I genuinely thought that I was going to leave the hospital with two sons and no wife. Images of a memorial service cascaded through my head, and it wasn't fair. It wasn't her time to go. It wasn't right. How could my new son do this to her? She needed to be here! I needed her desperately. For the first time in my life, I was mortally afraid – but not for my own life: for the life of another. For the love of my life. My beautiful bride, who chose me and decided to make a home with me and raise a family with me. And I was the one who got her pregnant! I did this to her! How could I have done this to her.

I nearly killed my wife.

The screams died down, and the baby was born, and we all celebrated, although tired as hell and beaten to an emotional pulp. It was joyful and terrifying and exuberant and wonderful. We cried, exhausted. Not tears of joy, but tears of relief. Somehow, in the midst of all of that, it was devoid of the same rejoicing we had the *first* time around. Whereas for the first birth my focus was 50% on my wife and 50% on my son, the second birth was 100% on my wife. I had an unshakeable feeling that she was going to suffer cardiac arrest, and I can still picture her lying on that bed, screams dying down, getting quieter now, and her fast, rapid breaths becoming white noise, blending into the steady *beeeeeeeeeeeeeep* of the flatline.

I have never been more afraid, and I hurt still at this typing.

It's over – I love you

My wife is ok. She made an excellent recovery, because, again, her body has been fused with an airplane black box or she's made of hardened lava. (You should see me try to lift her!) *thinks to self for a second* (I'm going to pay dearly for that comment.) Anyway, I finally connected with my son! I took him into my arms and kissed him, but he was far behind in the race of kiss receiving. I had kissed my wife and bawled into her hair through sobbing and tear-filled gratitude that she was still alive. It never occurred to me that the hospital was monitoring her too, and that for any sign of cardiac arrest they would have acted swiftly and accordingly. But she made it. And the hashtag warrior belongs to no other.

What I breathed into her ear. The things I said. *I need you. Brennan needs you. Asher needs you. Stay with me. Honey look at me. Honey listen to me.* I was absolutely powerless to take any of her fear and pain away. Me, the voiceover artist… had no voice. My voice meant nothing. When Asher came out, he actually ripped my wife, and they had to suture her up. I hear this is somewhat common in inductions, but whatever. I don't care about the statistics, I cared about saving my wife, and for the first time in my life I felt utterly powerless to do anything about anything except trust that in the dim reckoning of her mind, in the screaming pounding of her ears, she could hear the voiceover out there somewhere, gently, quietly urging her on and telling her she could do it. That voice was colored through blood and pain and anguish on June 12th, 2019, and it will never be the same.

===

And that's how Asher came into being. This little guy, all of *also* 6 pounds, 8 ounces and *also* of 20" long, was born in the exact same room at the hospital, but not in the exact same room of my heart. I didn't even know he had been born. I had difficulty connecting with him after he was born because I felt like he nearly killed my wife. Which is, of course, a ridiculous line of thought. Babies don't come equipped with shotguns or knives or poison. But what he did to her on his entry into this world caused her enormous pain that I will never forget and had a hard time parsing away from him.

However, all things settled, tranquility crept back in, and normalcy returned. I found that the little guy that I was holding, when my wife was catching up on sleep, was utterly beautiful. Utterly spellbinding, and an entirely different creature from Brennan. I would find myself just staring at him in confusion and wonder, knowing full well that he was mine, and yet wondering how in the world we ended up with two, and how were we suddenly a family of *four*. So crazy!

Over time, Asher grew. He latched properly, he nursed properly, and he grew. He had a smile worth a million bucks from early on. His glinting eyes sparkled. He was clearly intelligent. The trauma portal through which he was born imparted to him a wonderful sense of unflagging joy. Almost as if every single painful muscle contraction of my wife's uterus squeezed an extra helping of joy into him. He is named Asher, because that means 'happy' and 'blessed.' And he truly is.

Also, wonder of wonders, he is the exact opposite of Brennan. You can't plan this or make this stuff up, and I will never pretend to understand how it all works, but check this out:

- Brennan is a back sleeper; Asher is a tummy sleeper
- Asher wakes up happy; Brennan wakes up grumpy
- Brennan has brown hair; Asher has sandy blonde hair
- Asher is short and stout; Brennan is tall and slender
- Brennan is right-brain and creative; Asher is left-brain and scholarly
- Brennan is physical and a wrecking ball; Asher is careful and methodical
- Asher is medium-tempo; Brennan is a missile
- Brennan likes candy; Asher likes natural fruit
- Asher latched and nursed properly; Brennan didn't
- Brennan took almost a year to potty train; Asher picked it up right away
- Asher was born during a time of relative joy; Brennan was born during anxiety and fear

- Brennan is a winter baby; Asher is a summer baby
- Asher likes long sleeves; Brennan doesn't
- Brennan likes to wrestle; Asher doesn't want to
- Asher is messy; Brennan is neat and tidy
- Brennan looks a little like me; Asher looks nothing at all like me (but I do like to imply infidelity with my wife by shouting accusatorily, "But he *does* look like the mailman, explain that, honey!!!")

None of these are advantages or disadvantages on the part of either of my boys; they are simply profound differences between the two of them that are inexplicable. After all, they come from the same parents and the same parenting. But they utterly complement each other, and they are the other's foil. They perfectly balance each other out. And, as time went on, many of their interests would prove similar, i.e., Minecraft, Superman, Spider-Man, dinosaurs, etc., and, well, other things that nearly all boys like, like stomping in mud and stepping on worms.

Asher, A.J., our little "AshMan" is the second child we didn't exactly try for but are overjoyed in our heart of hearts to have been blessed with by God. He is utterly amazing, and Brennan is such a good big brother to him. They are great friends, and it warms our hearts to behold.

He has a super quick razor-sharp wit. For example, one time I was chasing after him when he was just a little guy running around shirtless in our home. I made the customary monster noises and growled, "Rawr, I'm gonna eat the first shirtless person I see!" To which Asher, now hiding behind mama, cleverly exclaimed, "Quick, Mama, take off your shirt!" I mean, you can't blame him, it's what an F-35 would do if it was being tailed: deploy chaff, and make the target hotter than they themselves are. Nice flyin,' son.

Another time, toddler Asher and I were sitting at the kitchen table talking about an (imaginary slight) I had taken. I was pretending to have my feelings hurt. After hearing only the small amount that he could tolerate, he tiredly threw his chin into his palm, shook his head, and grumbled, "You're always *drama*."

Asher is *very* smart. We think even gifted. He may in fact be a superhero. (We're awaiting the results from the bloodwork.) He is our little guy who understands his own foibles, loves to be silly, and is fantastically excellent in his schoolwork. And yet so much more. He truly is amazing.

Another thing about Asher is he has an incredibly sensitive spirit and *loathes* being in trouble. He can't stand it. There was a time when he was all of one year old in our new home. I was reclining on a beanbag chair in the living room and he walked up to me unannounced with one of my crocs in his hand. Without any kind of warning, he threw it right at my face at unawares, hitting me squarely in the nose. And *boy,* does that smart. I exclaimed – within reason – "Asher, ow! That hurt, why did you do that?" The answer, being, of course, that he is one, and has simply no clue why he did that because...again... *checks notes*... he is *one.* There is no other logical reason.

Well, little Asher quickly noted the change in Daddy's voice, but even before Daddy said a word, that little guy was convicted so deeply that he erupted into tears. He *knew,* instinctively, deep down in his little beating heart of hearts, that what he had done was wrong. He was so deeply convicted by it that he let loose a torrent of tears that washed all of Daddy's surprise and frustration away. I quickly pushed it all aside and said "aw, come here, Bub. It's okay." I stretched out my arms, and that little guy waded right into me and sunk into my consoling embrace that enveloped him and let him know that it truly was okay, it just surprised me.

All that to say that Asher can't stand being in trouble. He has *such* a tender heart that wants to do the right thing, and as such, he's often on the straight and narrow while Brennan is simultaneously on the wrong side of the tracks. He's going to be guardrails for him; he's going to help contain his tempest in life, we're sure of it.

Remember, Brennan is a button-pusher, and he can whine, protest, and talk back with the best of them? Well, Daddy doesn't like disobedience or talking back, so Daddy and Brennan have had plenty of tugs-o'-war where Daddy's voice may have gotten raised a bit in scolding Brennan. Do you know who has been on the sidelines for nearly every single one of those instances, watching, observing, cleverly taking notes and learning fully what *not* to do?

That's right. Our little AshMan. He doesn't want to
be in trouble, and he learns from brother's example
what *not* to do. Ha! Hopefully one day he'll learn
what *to* do from his brother's example. Asher is very
intuitive, and he processes the mistakes big brother
makes in order to not be in those same shoes. He is
very, very observant, and very, very smart. He wants
to make right decisions, he wants to bring peace, and
he wants to get along.

Some people have to learn the hard way. From what
I know of my eldest, that's Brennan. Others just stay
in compliance, and they proceed on a "to obey every
day in every way is the happy way" mindset, and
they avoid trouble. That's Asher. But I'm proud of
both of them.

Asher is also not an athlete; not a scholar; not a barrel
of energy. He's a snuggle buddy, my 6 o'clock
shadow, my partner, following me around with
stories that are filled with wonder and magic and *awe*.
He is *incredibly* talented at video games, and with
hand-eye coordination. I love him to pieces, and he is
our little surprise that completes our ensemble. He
loves his Daddy, and wants to hold *my* hand while

we're walking. He chooses me. I so love deeply that he chooses me.

TO ASHER:

I love you, Asher. You are my beloved son, in whom I am well pleased. You wake up singing. You bring light into dark places. Your name means happy and blessed, and you happily bless others. You talk with that telltale squint of your eyes, as if there's some beautiful squirrely mischief behind them. You deliver everything you say with a wink and a grin. You create drawings and crafts for others and deliver it to them unannounced, just because you thought they could use a little pick-me-up. I love how many times you tell me you love me throughout the day, and I want you to know that I never ever tire of it. It's the most beautiful sound in the whole world, and it comes from the most beautiful voice: yours.

You are my little shadow, following me around. You're my movie buddy, snuggling up next to me with your tiny little frame, leaning your head against mine. You play and cavort and jump, bouncing around on the couch near me to taunt me, trying to see if I can grab your leg before you get away, or will

I snag you and tickle you? Every single day has a game in it, every single hour has possibilities in it, and every single moment has joy stapled to it. I LOVE you for that, my Asher, my AJ, my AshMan.

You are my whole Earth, and everything in it.

Love,
Daddy

Chapter 4: Primrose

My book on Daddydom wouldn't be complete, really, if I didn't talk about our daughter.

You know, the four-legged one.

In 2012, my wife and I adopted an 8-week-old Lab / Chow / Shar Pei we named delightedly named Primrose (or, 'Miss Prim' for those regal galas she would attend). We were trying to conceive, but it hadn't happened yet, so we decided we'd settle on the next best thing and make our little twosome a threesome by bringing in a puppy.

We found this adorable pooch on Craigslist, drove 1.5 hours south to go get her, and though the adopter had said that she had all her vaccinations, we took her in straightaway to the vet the next day and gave her a clean bill of health, all the shots, all the tags, all the things.

Primrose utterly blessed our home. My wife likes to say, "she ushered us into parenthood." Because she truly did. Prim was our 'baby girl,' (another expression of my wife's) – and that was something that I'd never thought to call her. 'Baby girl?' How weird! I hadn't yet heard phrases like 'four-legged human' or things like that, but Prim certainly fit the bill. We had to love her, provide for her, feed her, clean up after her, train her, protect her, keep her healthy, and more. Being a dog owner is, in many respects, almost exactly like being a parent, so, *yes*, she ushered us into parenthood, and she did it with style and aplomb.

We *loved* Prim. She was such a sweet girl…

…for all of four and a half years.

At some point, Prim started to develop large balls under her jowls. You could feel them; they moved and were definitely growing. I suspected she might have an infection in her lymph nodes, and brought her in to the veterinarian. Prim was diagnosed with lymphoma in December of 2016, when Brennan was only ten months old. The vet took some bloodwork, ran it through the lab, and said he would call me with the results.

He finally called, and I didn't catch what he said; I hadn't heard him clearly at first because I was doing that thing where you partially listen to someone on the phone, but you're typing and getting things done on your computer at the same time, trying to multitask. I had to backup and pull the old, "Wait... what?" *What was that you said?*

When the vet repeated it, I was floored.

Prim had, at best, only six months to live. We could extend that with pharmaceuticals, but it would just be delaying the inevitable, and her quality of life would deteriorate if we did so. It was unavoidable in every respect: Prim was *going* to die.

I slowly made my way downstairs to tell my wife, and I bawled and sobbed the entire way. We were going to lose our baby girl, and we were unprepared. She had truly ushered us into parenthood, and now that we had our baby boy, we were going to lose our baby girl?

It wasn't right, and it wasn't fair.

Well, we loved on her, took care of her, gave her the necessary pharmaceuticals and healthy food – and lots of water for all the panting she was starting to do – but there was no staving this off. Her condition deteriorated, she would lie around, she wet the floor, she was always panting, and we had to make a choice. Do we prolong her suffering just because we can't bear to lose her? Or do we do the honorable thing, put her out of her misery, and lose her forever?

Just as the doc forecasted, Prim's six months were about up. There was only one choice. We loved her, and we didn't want to see her suffer.

We put Primrose to sleep on June 16th, 2017, two days before Father's Day. She slowly faded in front of our very eyes, and closed her eyes forever. Primrose was gone forever: she who had made us parents. She wasn't even five years old.

That Father's Day we rejoiced and mourned.

Two days later, my little boy and I were in the playroom of our former home. Brennan was nearing 1.5 years old, so he didn't really understand everything that had transpired with Prim. In his little innocent brain, he just knew that she was gone. He and I were in the playroom looking at pictures of Prim one morning, when he suddenly pulled his binky out of his mouth, waved at the screen, and said, "Bye bye."

I just stared at him in horror and shock, realizing the gravity of what he said, and though he scampered off to play, I just sat there, frozen in shock, marinating in my grief. I lost it, throwing the cover over my head so he wouldn't see me. I bawled. Brennan noted that I was crying, and he came over and pulled the blanket down over my face. Through my tears, I assured him that Daddy was okay.

I wasn't, but I would be. Losing a child is hard. Ernie Halter's song probably says it best:

I tried everything I could think of
No distraction could make this feeling end
But if I could go back

I wouldn't change a thing
I'd love you all over again

Nothing could take away
Nothing could take away
Nothing could take away
This beautiful ache
This beautiful ache

Your memory is all I have to hold on to
Our yesterday will not let me go
But if I could go back
I wouldn't change a thing
I'd love you all over again

Nothing could take away
Nothing could take away
Nothing could take away
This beautiful ache
This beautiful ache[1]

To this very day, I can't even listen to this song. The
opening piano chords absolutely slay me. My heart
goes out to anyone who has ever lost a son or
daughter, especially while young. I have two friends
who have both lost daughters, and I've watched them

walk through their ache with dignity and grace…it's something I don't know that I could do without *tremendous* help from Above.

It took a great amount of time for me to recover from the loss of Primrose. We got her as a puppy and we loved her with every ounce of our being as her parents. We watched her grow. We laid with her and stroked her fur. We laughed and played with her. She was our baby girl. She lives now only in our hearts, and we will never forget her.

DEAR PRIMROSE:

Thank you, from the bottom of our hearts, for ushering us into parenthood, and for letting us love you. We are better, far better parents, for loving you. I miss you every single day, my baby girl.

Love,
Daddy

Chapter 5: Just Any Dad

Pardon the profanity, but there's a phrase I have to share with you out of one of my all-time favorite movies, *Parenthood*, and to edit it down would be to do the gravity of it a disservice. It's voiced by Keanu Reeve's character, Tod, as he is reflecting on the poor fathering he received, and the poor fathering that his protégé, Gary, has received from *his* father. Here it is:

"You know, Mrs. Buckman, you need a license to buy a dog. You need a license to drive a car - hell, you even need a license to catch a fish. But they'll let any butt-reaming asshole be a father." - Tod Higgins, Parenthood (1989).

The sad reality – and it is *truly* sad – is that this utterly true. Statistics show that Father's Day generates significantly more collect calls from

inmates, sometimes 27% more than Mother's Day.[2]
Why is that? Male inmates are calling out to their
families, their children, their mothers. So many men
in jail... children without active fathers in their
lives... sons without role models... daughters
without protectors. It's a brutal life-sucking pattern
that has far-reaching consequences and tends to
contribute to a repeat pattern: those sons could grow
up and be absent fathers as well, or even incarcerated
themselves.

Fathers are underrated. They provide life; they are
the carriers. Anyone can be a father; but it takes a
special type of person to be a dad. If you want to
become a better dad, I *highly* recommend picking up a
copy of Ryan Holiday's "The Daily Dad." It is
massively inspirational. I go through it every day and
each day, I learn – or relearn – something important
and indispensable from it.

Speaking of quotes, I'd like to share with you some of
the most inspiring quotes about fatherhood. As an
author, I can only say so much... but these time-
honored quotes say more than I ever could. I pray
that these will inspire you as they did me.

"A good father is one of the most unsung, unpraised, unnoticed, and yet one of the most valuable assets in our society." -Billy Graham

"The presence and involvement of a father is unlike anything else in the universe. That's because dads mimic what our heavenly Father does for us, His children — He protects, shelters, comforts and loves."
-Joe Battaglia

"Dads are most ordinary men turned by love into heroes, adventurers, story-tellers, and singers of song.
-Pam Brown

"My father gave me the greatest gift anyone could give another person, he believed in me." -Jim Valvano

"A father's presence is more important than a father's provision." -Paul Strozier

"The nature of impending fatherhood is that you are doing something you're unqualified to do, and then you become qualified while doing it." –John Green

"A father carries pictures where his money used to
be."
-Steve Martin

"I cannot think of any need in childhood as strong as
the need for a father's protection." -Sigmund Freud

"No man I ever met was my father's equal, and I
never loved any other man as much." -Hedy Lamarr

"When my father didn't have my hand, he had my
back."
-Linda Poindexter

"The heart of a father is the masterpiece of nature."
-Antoine Francois Prevost

"Dad: A Son's first hero, a daughter's first love."
-Unknown

I've met a lot of dads in my lifetime. There are many
that I've been less than impressed by. I even have
one in my own family that has, in one way or
another, literally expressed to me that he'd rather be
doing other things than being a dad or husband.
Breaking his kids' toys in front of them. Barking

orders and shouting at his *and* my kids. It's been
upsetting to witness. Now, I'm a realist: a good yell
releases stress, frustration, and pent-up anger. If
your kids are actively being disobedient and not
listening, something has to get their attention.

But seriously, have you ever tried *whispering* instead?
I am not joking. There have been a few (read:
92,859,253 times and counting) times where my kids
are not listening to me; they're knee-deep in whatever
fun they've concocted, and they're utterly engrossed
in it. In those moments, Dad doesn't really exist; he's
some presence on the far periphery, observing only.
They've completely tuned me out. And raising my
voice didn't help. So? I went in the reverse direction.
A slow whisper, just on the edge of hearing, that
creeps into their subconscious and tickles at them.
Said the quiet dad to the little boys.... Do you hear what I
hear? It's atypical; it's attention-getting. They stop
what they're doing and listen up. Oh, not right away,
I grant you, but there have been plenty of times
where it's worked, because it was the very opposite
of what they expected or were conditioned to. In the
middle of all their noise comes this deafening
whisper that is just different enough to wrest their

attention away from their recreation, and get them to pay attention.

My goal is to get their attention through whispering more than yelling.

The point in all this is that dads are fundamental, intrinsically critical and utterly formative in a child's development. Notice that I didn't say *fathers*. I said *dads*. There's an intimacy there that is not necessarily present in the word *fathers*. Biologically, I have the capacity to pass on life and produce children. But producing children in and of itself does not make me a dad. That only makes me a biological father. Kids don't need biological fathers; they need *dads*.

There are incredible stories about fathers being dads that are so heartwarming. So encouraging. So wonderful to know that there are men out there willing to step up and be the man their child(ren) need them to be. I recently stumbled upon several accounts at Readers Digest here.[3] Check them out!

The greatest thing a Daddy can do to show their children that they are important is pay attention to them. Be involved with them. Give of your own

time. Put down your phone (I'll talk about this in the
next chapter.) Sacrifice of your own interests to
ensure that you engage with theirs. For dads, this
means getting up out of your easy chair and putting
down the newspaper to be intentional about crafting
with them… watching a fun and interactive show
with them… reading a story to them… putting a
puzzle together with them… playing games with
them (we have *great* games like 'Invisible Kid' where
they tap me on the shoulder, I pretend to be surprised
and slowly turn to look for them, but they turn with
me and stay behind me and I can't see them, which
begets me exclaiming "Huh? So weird… I thought I
felt something… I could have sworn someone was
there…" and then they tap me on the *other* shoulder,
and round and round we go) … going for walks…
teaching them push-ups… exercising with them…
training them to ride a bike… going outside to play
make-believe… playing board games or card games
with them, and when they beat you, make a huge
deal out of it with feigned, overblown outrage and
incredulity… watching them do their little stunts and
performances… rescheduling passable private
activities in favor of actively engaging with them…
intentionally scheduling family activities… going
places together… taking off work. Making *memories.*

Playing with them, roughhousing with them and watching them test their little budding strength against you, is one of the single greatest privileges a Daddy can enjoy. In fact, one of the greatest things you will find in life is sticking your finger deep in their necks, evoking the beautiful and lifegiving chuckle they make as they crinkle up and try to wriggle out of it. Or the sheer terror you send through them as you chase after them with monster roars and growls as they shriek in terror and run for their lives. Let me tell you, sending that primal fear into their little bodies feeds my very soul.

The measure of a dad is judged not by how much he provides nor how much he protects, but by how much he *participates*.

Fathers inseminate women and sometimes move on. *Dads* stick around and get involved. Fathers biologically reproduce and bail. *Dads* beneficially relate and bond.

Tod in *Parenthood* had it right. They'll let any man be a father. Only those filled with character and integrity decide to step up, abandon the father mantle and step into the play clothes of Dad. As my friend Holt likes to say, 'Dads are in charge of fun.' He's so right. We're in charge of bringing play, silliness (bring on the Dad jokes, baby!), recreation, wrestling, and so much more into our home. It isn't just about providing a nice home and spoiling them with everything their little hearts desire (and their little hearts desire *checks notes* yep… a LOT). It's about wanting to get down on our hands and knees and let them ride us like a horse. About wrestling them and allowing them to get the upper hand. About building things with them and together beholding the wonder of our mutual creation. About playing with them and being silly. About using our strength not for threat displays or cockiness or strutting our stuff to show how much we've provided, but using our strength to impute it into them: to give it away…

To take our strength and give it to them.

Dads are *so* important. And of course moms are too! Moms and Dads, together in a marital partnership, are undeniably formative in a child's understanding of how the world works, of what love looks like, etc.

But Dads hold a special place in a child's understanding of their own humanity, from their role in the pecking order to their place in this world. It's our job to communicate value, to affirm, to strengthen, to build up. Not only to provide and protect, but also to play.

TO MY SONS:

I am so sorry for all the times I've been a father and not a Dad to you. You needed a warm and approachable Dad; I was a cold and removed father. I love you so much, from my heart to yours, and I wish that you could peel back the layers and see inside my heart and know how utterly valuable you are to me... what great worth you hold in my heart... how eternally proud I am of you and that tiny little demonstration of charity you showed the other day, that you didn't have to... *but you did.* You went the extra mile and you showed your quality: the very highest.

There have been so many times in my fatherhood where I've regretted how self-absorbed I've been while I strove to provide for our family. I am so proud of you for patiently waiting on the sidelines for me to return out of my own game so that you could play yours. Forgive me.

May *I* be the one on the sidelines always cheering *you* on. May you outlast me, outperform me, outsucceed me, outrace me, outpace me, out*everything* me as I cheer you on, because I'm your biggest fan. After all, I'm not just any father.

I'm your Dad.

Love,
Daddy

Chapter 6: Dad's Greatest Enemy

Tangina Barrons, played by Zelda Rubenstein in *Poltergeist*, perhaps said it best.

There's one more thing. A terrible presence is in there with her. So much rage, so much betrayal. I've never sensed anything like it. I don't know what hovers over this house, but it was strong enough to punch a hole into this world and take your daughter away from you. It keeps Carol Anne very close to it and away from the spectral light. It *lies* to her, it tells her things only a child could understand. It has been using her to restrain the others. To her, it simply *is* another child. To us, it is the Beast.[4]

While the 'beast' in my life is not quite as spectral as the demonic lifeforce in *Poltergeist*, it's perhaps best epitomized by a 6.5" high by 3" wide rectangle with a little Apple logo on the back.

I'm talking about my iPhone. Guys, let's be honest: how many times have we signaled that we need to go to the bathroom when our family is all home together, only to bring that little device in there with us, and, before we knew it, our short bathroom break turns into a half-hour of browsing, watching reels, and doomscrolling?

But here's the kicker. The greatest enemy to my relationship with my kids might be *personified* by my iPhone, but let's be honest. It's not Tangina Barrons' literal demon, but it's another one: far more clever, far more erosive, far more toxic to my relationship with my kids.

It's the demon of *Distraction.*

I know, in my heart of hearts, that one day one or both of my sons are going to say to me, "Why are you on your phone so much?" Or, "how come you're always on your iPhone, Dad?" And they would be right… I'm constantly whipping out my iPhone to check for notifications of any and all kinds: book sales, important emails, Facebook notifications, and other Pavlovian temptations and bells that my eyes, ears and heart are conditioned and trained to look out for. There's something ego-stroking about notifications on my phone: someone cared enough to interact with me, and I want it.

Reread what I just wrote, please. *There's something ego-stroking about notifications on my phone: someone cared enough to interact with me, and I want it.*

Isn't that true of our children? They want their ego stroked. They want someone to interact with them. *They want to feel valuable.*

Are there down times in our home? Sure. Are there times where the kids get screen time and they don't want or need to be distracted by Mom or Dad? Of course. Are there times where they need to do their chores or their reading? Absolutely. Are there times where they will be out at school, or asleep? Most definitely. Can I use those times to stick my nose in my phone?

Without a doubt.

In many schools these days, at least in Washington state[5], there are new rules implemented about students surrendering their phones upon entry, so that there's no chance they'll be distracted during class. Yes, some of those rules center around preventing cheating, but make no mistake: smartphones, especially for young, impressionable teens, are a huge source of distracting Pavlovian bells that can become incredibly addictive; something that must be surrendered.

But if the kids have to surrender their phones during the day in school so that they pay attention, shouldn't we as parents be forced to comply with a similar edict in the evening when they're home, so that *we* pay attention? A 'no phones after 5pm' rule, for as long as the kids are awake?

I've always prided myself on responding quickly to texts and emails. It's something that has really enabled me to become more successful in business. But I often wonder what kind of image I'm putting out there: *Aaron Ryan responded to my email practically before I even sent it! Wow, that guy is FAST!* But what message am I *really* conveying in doing so? That I have no life? That I'm glued to my phone? And if I have kids, shouldn't there be a delay in my response because that would imply that I'm at least *remotely* involved with them, or my wife, engrossed in their lives rather than my own?

It's a balancing act, to be sure. You do have your own life, and you are your own person, and you do have things to attend to. There are plates spinning around you at all times, demanding your attention and calling for your concentration and awareness.

As an author, I struggle with the promotion I constantly have to do that requires my focus to be on always trying to sell my books. I struggle with the amount of time away I've had to take at vendor markets and craft fairs, out there setting up a booth, selling books, and taking time away from my family. During those times, I can neither provide nor protect. I can only pray. Pray for their welfare, their safety, their obedience, their fun, their growth… while I'm away.

But if I'm really being honest with myself, it was this way with voiceovers… it was this way with wedding videography… it was this way with multimedia production… it's been this way *ever since I got an iPhone and had access to the Internet on the go.* The industry isn't the problem; my focus is.

Sometimes, life seems to be all about trying to just make sure that you stay on top of everything… making sure that everything gets taken care of and that you don't miss anything. But we should never 'miss' our kids. *They* are the everything that we need to stay on top of. Everything else is secondary. Don't get distracted from the *real* responsibility.

There are exceptions of course. I'm an author, but I'm also a full time voiceover artist. As the latter, there have been times where we've scheduled a family vacation and, before we left, I was informed by my agent that I booked a job, and the client wants a directed session with me – *while I'm on vacation!* That means I have to bring my portable sound booth with me (yes, they really make these) and I have to carve out precious time from my precious schedule with my precious kids (and my precious wife!) and do that session.

Or, it's a summer day, and we're just about to head out to the water park… when a client says that I messed up something in their recordings and they need the corrected audio right away. There are sometimes exceptions that are work-related that you simply can't get around.

It's the same with being an author. Being an author comes with its share of distractions as well. As it should! It's my job... and if I don't work, I don't get paid... if I don't get paid, we don't have a house. Naturally, there needs to be a defined schedule that allows me to work, and that must be respected by all. But if I'm sitting and writing, and my kids come out to the shop and burst into my office, that doesn't mean that work goes on. No. *Life* goes on, and I can *usually* put everything on hold and pay attention to them for as long as they're in my office, treating them as special and welcome visitors. Life won't end if I do that. On the contrary: it *continues.*

Now, they know just as I do that if I'm sitting in a podcast interview, they need to wait. If I'm in the last chapter of a book and I've already stated that I need time to focus and finish, they need to respect those boundaries and give me the time needed to actually get things done. They learn this in time of course. All kids do: routine is something they understand; whether it's bath night or church on Sunday or school. They get it.

But as a Dad, the reverse is true as well, and you can
bet your bottom dollar that if you have kids, life is
never going to go exactly as planned. Once I was out
in the shop working when Brennan burst in, panting.
Asher had fallen against the coffee table and split
open his ear. We had to take him to the emergency
room to get stitches. In such moments, everything
gets dropped.

Or, when Asher was a little guy, we had friends over
for dinner, and were engaged outside in a fun and
lively conversation on the patio. Asher was on the
potty, and needed us to wipe him (which is every
parent's absolute favorite activity, bar none). Being
outside, we couldn't hear him calling for us inside.
Thankfully, the little guy was smart enough to have
Alexa make a house-wide announcement, and before
we knew it, we all heard the Echo proclaiming,
"Mama, Dada, I need to wipe!"

Gross, but true. So, our fun and lively conversation
was put on hold so that we could attend to our kiddo.

Life gets put on hold, and we get distracted by our
kiddos. *That* distraction is the right one. We're

washing dishes, and our child needs us to open their juice bottle. We're paying bills, and our child needs us to look at the incredible drawings they just made. We're working on the car, and our child needs us to help them with pronunciation of a word in a book. We're in a phone call, and our child needs us to enter the code on his iPad to extend his screen time.

Life is replete with little distractions that take you off the rails either momentarily or for a great amount of time. As a Dad, for me it's all about balancing all those plates that I'm spinning, so that none of them falls. You become an octopus; you really do: spinning all those plates all the time and ensuring that they all remain aloft, so that nothing shatters.

But back to that big demon, for a moment…

When I decide to hole up in the bathroom and doomscroll, I've just abandoned all those plates, and enabled a potentially gigantic mess for myself to clean up out there. I've surrendered all my responsibilities – and my privileges - with my kids and my wife, to selfishness. To my own whims, desires, and need for isolation. If I truly needed to hit the bathroom, that's fine. But it's a temporary visit;

not a forwarding of my address. I need to remember
that.

Let's be frank. Should you have as much time as you
want to poop? Science would agree with me that if
you don't poop, you're in for a world of hurt. Take
the time you need. It's all about balance. If you're
going in there to do your duty and get it done, a little
light reading doesn't hurt. But know where to draw
the line. Finding yourself endlessly flicking that
thumb, spoon-feeding yourself all those useless reels
and ingesting news article after news article, or
overdosing on news, takes you away from your
biggest source of news, standing just outside. (Or,
just *inside* the bathroom door, if you're our family:
our kids simply don't grasp the importance of
'privacy' still…). In all of this, I'm talking to myself
here.

As with all things, it's all about balance. Don't beat
yourself up if you need to take a little 'me time' here
and there. We all do. It's important for self-health
and personal maintenance. But don't retreat and
isolate. *Never* retreat and isolate. Take some time
away to get done what you need to, but don't retreat
and isolate. Again, balance.

My biggest enemy is Distraction, capital D, for sure. I owe it to my children to be focused on them, and to show them that they are the whole earth to me.

And do you know what's worse than not being there at all? Being there and yet *not* being there. That's far worse. It would be better if you weren't there at all, because now, you're a visual reminder of something they can't have: quality time with Dad. You're physically present, but emotionally, spiritually, and intellectually absent. They can see you, but they can't touch you, and there's nothing that you're giving them. I have been guilty of this as well, and I always need to remember to not just be there, but to really *be* there. Be present, but also be *present.*

Let's get rid of the enemy, of Distraction, *yesterday.* I propose a straight-up exchange, for a daddy's greatest ally, *Delight.* Let us *delight* in our children, giving unsparingly and unreservedly, putting the brakes on all things minutiae, and utterly delighting in them. If there's one thing my kids could say about me, its this: when they talk, I smile and listen.

DEAR BRENNAN AND ASHER:

Forgive me for all the times where you've stood there patiently waiting for me to stop tapping my phone. Forgive me for the number of times you've called my name once… twice… THREE TIMES!! to get my attention. The word *Dad* should have been a klaxon within my hull that snapped me to military attention and made me pay you the respect you deserve. Forgive me for all the times where I've felt I've needed to be out and about, trying to provide for my family.

While having those resources have been important – and I've needed to provide for my family while I've chased my dreams doing so – I confess that many of those times I've done it for the image more than providing for my family, and for that, I'm so sorry, my sons. I want you to know how much you beat within my heart. I want you to know that you are everything to me, and I will always try harder to be utterly present for you.

You are my whole Earth.

I love you,
Daddy

Chapter 7: Bag of Tricks

Every family is different. Variety truly is the spice of
life. You learn things from other parents and other
families: how they operate, how they push their kids,
what rules they enforce, what their priorities are,
what their downtime looks like, what they do on their
days off, how they discipline, how they talk to their
kids, how they help their kids solve problems and
empower them, how they care for them, how each
parent understands each of their children, etc.

I used to watch my friends get married and have kids
and feel totally lost in the tempest that is their life
now, with all the frenzy happening all around them.
The mess. The toys on the floor. The unkempt
bedrooms. The crayons everywhere. The different
programming they now watch on TV. Their sudden
changes in movie tastes (read: only anything G-rated

or below). How mature they got. The list goes on
and on.

Now I understand completely. There are humans,
and then, there are *parents*. These last ones are
otherwise known as *superhumans*. They are charged
with the greatest responsibility of all: raising up the
young, taking care of them, protecting them from all
things PG-rated and above.

How they all do it, however, is vastly different from
one roof to the next.

One thing I learned from a neighbor is how they
practice 'Gratitude Day.' It's something where they
only have rice to eat, and they practically eat it
unflavored. All they get, all day, is rice. And water.
But.... *rice.* And that's all.

Rice.

So, we adopted it. We've only done it a few times,
but through the growling of our tummies and the
yearnings of our taste buds, we are reminded that so
many in this world go without. Talk about a lesson
in how to be grateful for what you have, right?

One of the greatest axioms that came to me one day as a parent is, "Be grateful for what you do have, not angry about what you don't." That's something I repeatedly find myself telling Brennan. He needs to hear that because he has a tendency to pine for what he wants, and if he doesn't get it, he can sulk.

Without guilt-tripping him, I try to remind him that there are so many little boys and girls that will go to bed tonight hungry. Or with no roof over their head. Or without a single toy. I try to remind him (and Asher) that they have *so* much. Really, in America, they are spoiled more or less by default because the provision quotient here is astronomical compared to some third world countries. We have *so* much. I've even taken the extreme of showing them starving African children with distended stomachs and bulging eyes staring out through bony skeletons. They need to see what they have, *really* see it, and understand how tremendously much they've been given by comparison. It's a hard lesson to teach *and* a hard lesson to witness, but it is genuinely eye opening.

Gratitude Day helps accomplish that as well. They learn the value of self-sacrifice. We've only done it a few times, but it does leave the tummy grumbling and it does remind us how much we really have. A poor, homeless, starving child can't just amble over to a kitchen cupboard and pull out some fruit snacks, Nilla wafers, Saltine crackers, or yogurt pouch. They don't need to choose *which* toy to play with, because they have *no* toys. They have to pray that they'll get water soon; they don't get to open the fridge and *decide* between water, lemonade, orange juice, apple juice, or hot cocoa. It's water, only water... and often, sadly, it's *maybe* water.

We're spoiled here in the United States, and I want my boys to know that without a doubt. I want them to be grateful for what they do have, not angry about what they don't. Nothing makes me prouder than when one of my boys sacrifices something he has and decides that, because there's only one left of whatever it is, brother can have it. Or Mommy can have it. Or Daddy can. They can go without. I am *so* proud of them when they see the value of self-sacrifice.

One thing the boys do daily is record something in a 'Gratitude Journal.'[6] It's just for kids, but it allows them to draw a picture of who or what they're grateful for, write what they appreciated about today, what they give thanks for, etc.. It's a living document, and a track record of them choosing to give thanks for something in their lives. I think this is indispensable and *so* essential at their age!

Something else I've recently instituted is 'No Parents Day.' This is a day meant to foster independence on their part. To teach them that we won't always be around. If they need to open up a juice box, they'll need to do it on their own. If they want macaroni and cheese for lunch, they'll need to make it on their own. If Asher wants to get into their Spiderman costume, he'll need to zip himself up. If Brennan wants to pour himself some apple juice, he'll need to get it out of the fridge and carefully pour it himself.

Mommy and Daddy won't be around forever. That's the truth. Our boys know that. And the more we empower them to live without us, the better job we've done. The more dependent they are on us, the more we've failed them. It is our duty and our job to raise independent kids, and it is our job to prepare them to live independently from us.

Now, 'No Parents Day' doesn't mean they get to do whatever they want. We observe, and we ensure that what they're doing falls within the parameters of good behavior. They can't just sit around and watch TV all day, neglecting to brush their teeth, remaining in their underwear. They can't just eat garbage. They must demonstrate that they can take care of themselves and each other. I find this 'day' invaluable, and I look forward to doing this as much as possible with them. It's also utterly enjoyable to see how they manage without us.

Yet another is a game we play while driving, and it's the 'Pay Attention Game.' It is, quite simply, a challenge for them to make a mental note of everything they see, hear, feel, and experience in thirty seconds, and then they have to close their eyes for *another* thirty seconds during which they recount everything they can remember from the first thirty. Whoever gets the most points (one point per observation) wins! The point of this exercise is to get them to pay attention to *everything* around them... to be observant... to be *present*.

An area where we have failed them? Well, here goes. This is something that I regret, because I'm sure

there's something in our Bag of Tricks we haven't
availed ourselves of yet. But I'm confident it's in
there.

Brennan has always had an issue with falling asleep,
as well as being afraid of the dark, and he needs night
lights and white noise or soft music playing. But he
has also grown accustomed to us staying in the room
with him until he falls asleep. That's an area where
my wife and I have both failed him. We need to kiss
him goodnight, give him the creature comforts he
needs such as his galaxy light, his soft music, and
then *just leave the room*. But we don't. He is
responsible for his own sleep cycle, and he is
responsible for developing a feeling of independent
security, and he is responsible for falling asleep on his
own. The more we teach him that *we* are responsible
for helping him fall asleep, the less we equip him,
and more dependent on us he'll be. He needs to be
responsible in his own right.

One thing my wife implemented during the summer
a few years ago, when Brennan was perhaps 6 and
Asher 3, is Quiet Time. This was a period of time
where they were sent to their rooms to read, be quiet,
relax, untether, unwind, be calm, and perhaps even

nap. It was healthy on multiple levels, because it allowed Mama to get some work done and catch up, while the boys got a chance to be by themselves, learn independence, learn how to calm themselves, relax and untether, improve their reading, etc.

Quiet time is invaluable, and we still rely on it. It's wonderful to see them go up to their rooms, and to hear them over whatever baby monitors we have left) reading quietly to themselves, humming, or whatever, in order to pass the time enjoyably and quietly. It's not a banishment; it's a right and a privilege.

Quiet Time works for everyone. Why do you think Italians still enjoy a *siesta* each afternoon? Why do cultures in the Middle East and Asia take similar midday breaks? Why do those in the Philippines take *idlip*, a short nap inherited from Spanish colonizers? Why does Greece observe "Hours of Common Silence"? It's intuitive – we're hardwired to need rest!

Apart from things like these, our bag of tricks includes time-honored phrases that I'm now realizing my parents said to me. Life truly does come full circle! The axiom I mentioned earlier about being grateful for what you have is something that I think has intrinsic value for teaching them gratitude.

Gratitude is *so* important for kids as they grow. We're not raising Veruca Salts here. We want kids who are grateful and demonstrate it. Brennan, by the way, has impeccable manners and is *so* good with saying *please* and *thank you*.

Some axioms I've used on my kids:

- *Be grateful for what you have, not angry about what you don't*
- *Listen; because someday, listening will save your life.*
- *Listening shows you really care*
- *He who has the most friends wins*

I've got more, but I don't need to impress you. Suffice it to say that I hear myself recycling phrases used on me by my parents, I make new ones, and I pull still others out of a bag of tricks that enables me to work my magic of affirmation and instruction over my kids so that they will (hopefully) grow up correctly and uprightly.

But hear me now, and know this definitively. There is absolutely *nothing* greater that I could use on them than one little thing.

It's called *Prayer*.

I believe in God. I believe in Jesus Christ. I believe in The Holy Spirit. And as such, I believe that they are able to do *far* more than I ever could in my sons' lives, in their hearts, and in their souls, to steer them correctly, to take care of them, to protect and provide for them, to love them in ways that I can't, and to ensure that they know how valuable they really are.

But there's yet another aspect to it. I remember having lunch with my dad in 2000 at a restaurant, and he said something that stuck with me. He said, "At one point I just had to release you three boys (his sons) to the Lord, or I would go insane." There is *so* much power and truth in that. When you commit your children to prayer, and consistently, regularly, obediently pray for them, there is a transference of custodial responsibility over them. There is a bold move of surrender that commits them to Greater Care.

No matter how hard I work to take care of my kids and to try to ensure that they grow up well, there is someone who can do it WAY better than I can. I can't possibly keep my fingers on that many pulses. I can't possibly control them and ensure that they do the right things their entire lives. If I tried, like my dad, I would go insane.

The only one who can do all that is God.

The greatest tool I have in my bag of tricks is nothing I can use *on* them; prayer is something I can only use *over* them. I can come up with all kinds of clever axioms and bumper sticker phrases that will hopefully make an impression, but its not the words directed at *them* that make the difference; it's the words petitioned to *The Lord* that will ultimately make the difference. I *love* this excerpt:

> *Pray for me; more things are wrought by prayer*
> *Than this world dreams of.*
> *Wherefore, let thy voice*
> *Rise for me like a fountain night and day.*
> *For what are men better than sheep or goats,*
> *That nourish a blind life within the brain,*
> *If, knowing God, they lift not hands of prayer,*

Both for them and for those who call them friend?
For so the whole round earth is every way
Bound by gold chains about the feet of God.[7]

"For so the whole round Earth – *remember that* – is every way bound by gold chains about the feet of God."

They are my whole Earth… my whole round Earth, in every way, bound by gold chains about the feet of God. He sees them, He hears them, He loves them. I must pray for them. More things are wrought by prayer than this world dreams of. I must therefore let my voice rise for them like a fountain night and day. For what am I, better than a sheep or a goat, that nourishes a blind life within the brain, if even though I know God, I don't lift hands of prayer for my sons?

They are my whole Earth. I *must* pray for them. *That…* is the greatest tool in my bag of tricks.

DEAR BRENNAN AND ASHER:

You have no idea how often and fervently I pray for you. You have no idea how much I lift you to the Father. He loves you far more than I would ever be capable of doing. Learn from me, grow under my watchful embrace, but know that I am only your earthly father. There is your Heavenly Father, THE Father, over all of us, and He loves you with an everlasting love.

In Jesus' Name,
AMEN

Chapter 8: Legacy

I keep a daily journal for my beloved sons. It's one of the things that I'm most proud of. It's a record of their lives, undimmable, immovable, unchangeable, immutable, forever, and I've done it nearly every single day of their lives since Brennan was two months old in May of 2016. It's something that will be the greatest gift I have ever given them.

An elderly, maternal role model in my life, Jeanne, once set this same example for me by doing the same thing for her 'kids' in the college group at my old church. I had no idea! She showed them to me when we reconnected in 2007, and it blew me away. They were utterly precious, they were expansive, and they were rich with prayer and blessing. She recorded *so* many journals for me out of love for me, care for me, and a desire that I would do right and grow well.

Her mind was on me. Her love was over me. I know my Journal For My Beloved Sons will mean the same to my own kids.

That journal is *legacy*. Some other ways we celebrate legacies in our home:

- There are pictures all over. Some might wonder what happened to the walls (answer: what walls?) and do we even understand what white space is? (answer: those words sound like they should mean something to me, but I'm coming up empty.) Our kids are everywhere, and there are memories of them everywhere.
- We have school photo frames that allow for not just that school year's photo to be displayed, but also allows you to store all the previous photos in the frame itself. Finish one year, move that photo inside the frame (which is kind of like a book), and keep it forever, inserting the new, current photo into the visible portion that hands on the wall. But we keep all of them.
- We have tubs devoted to each son, loaded with certificates of achievement, report cards,

yearbooks, artwork, crafts, special tributes to them by teachers or friends, keepsakes, and memorabilia that attests to where they were at that year and at that stage.

- We have the obligatory height chart on the wall, marking off their growth development milestones.

- We have audio recordings in our iPhones that go back years: random voice captures of each son saying different things in different circumstances at different locations, and they are all so precious. I'll never forget when my wife sent me one such voice memo recording of my toddler Brennan saying "Dada, come home!" when I was at a men's function at our church. It broke me. It was so sweet, that tiny little voice and that heartfelt plea. I so wanted to be with him instead of there. Another favorite is when little Asher is trying to pronounce, with much verve and enthusiasm, complicated dinosaur names that are beyond his paygrade. Hilariously adorable.

- We take a monthly picture of them on the same exact boppy pillow and blanket that we've been taking pictures of them on every single month since they were born. To date,

Brennan has 118 monthly photos, and Asher has 78. We can scroll through all of them in succession and witness, clearly, their monthly growth. Oh how much change they go through in a single month, especially right after birth! We can behold how their little bodies stretch out and start to extend well beyond the (what once was) gigantic boppy pillow, and when they start to stretch even beyond the blanket. They grow right before our eyes. We take this every month on the 12th, because Brennan was born on February 12th, and Asher was born on June 12th. (Incidentally, that also brings my wife and I together because I proposed to her on June 12th, 2011, and we were married in 2012. We're also Seahawks fans, aka, '12's,' so '12' has special significance in our family.)

- Every year on the morning of my sons' birthdays, I take the same picture with them: me, shirtless, holding them up while they wear a white T-Shirt. We take a selfie against the wall. One of these days that picture is going to switch, and it will be a strapping young man in that picture holding up an aging father. I honestly can't wait for that switch, mostly because they're getting freaking heavy. I once saw this on CNN[8] and it moved me so deeply that I resolved to do it every year with my own boys.

- I keep all their little crafts they make for me on Father's Day... their stick figure drawings of them and me. Someday I'll have them all framed or put into a book. (I'm an author; I have some experience making books.)

- We have, at the time of this book's publishing, 23,492 photos and videos of our sons in an album dating back to June 19th, 2015 when we first found out we were pregnant. *Twenty-three thousand four-hundred ninety-two photos and videos.* I swear they are the most documented thing in history next to 9/11.

Our sons matter to us. They are *legacy* for us. They are deeply cherished and loved, and we want them to know how important they are. The amount of time invested in them by us is, in turn, its own legacy. A legacy of love, of commitment, of valuing them utterly. They will carry that valuation through life with them.

Brennan, as I mentioned, is an incredible 3D crafter. He *loves* making things out of paper and crafting them into multi-dimensional works of art. But should we ever accidentally throw one of those crafts away in our routine house-cleanings? Oh my. Here come the waterworks. That kid is *leveled*. His eyes shine, and he's filled with an aching sadness. He doesn't assume that it pains us that we can't find it, and I'm *positive* he doesn't think that we didn't value it – or him – but nonetheless, it's a loss that hits him roughly, and is felt deeply.

Make no mistake, we try to keep everything we can. But we are not of limitless real estate. We can only keep so much, and then, the overflow needs to fill another tub, and/or we have to make room in the existing tub and throw out what we discern might be aging or dated. The same goes for our occasional 'purges' where the kids help us purge old toys to give to Goodwill or Value Village so that others can enjoy their old, unwanted toys. We *have* to occasionally throw out stuff. But it doesn't mean that it's not hard to part with.

We're very interested in lasting legacy, our family. In fact, all of my careers as an independent freelancer have been about legacy. *All* of them. Corporate and especially wedding videography, memorial videos, videotape transfer to DVD, audio cleanup and preservation, voiceovers, and now, especially, authoring – all of them have been about leaving a footprint down through the ages, making something that lasts and attests to the worth of its subject or content. We love legacy here, and we love leaving it, and we love celebrating it. We know that one day, we're going to look back and find something that we had forgotten about, and it's going to open a Pandora's Box of rich memories.

Here come our own waterworks.

I still tear up watching my boys' births. I still tear up watching the video of my proposal to my wife, or at our wedding video when she walks down the aisle. Just like I do when I watch any good story in movie form. We are storytellers, all of us, and all humans love a good story. We celebrate stories because they hold great and cherished memories for all of us.

When I got engaged to my wife, my mom fell in love with her. She loves my wife dearly. She ended up making her a gift to celebrate our engagement, and to introduce Janine to her son, whom she was proud of. She made a beautiful photo album loaded to the rafters with photos, report cards, news articles, book reports, certificates of achievement, mementos, keepsakes, and Lord knows what else, but all of it was a testament, a time capsule if you will, of who I was at the time, and who my wife would be marrying. (I just thank God there was nothing salacious or incriminating in there.)

In truth, I was *floored.* I had no idea she still had any of that stuff! She had kept *so* much paperwork and other things from my childhood because it was sacred to her, and now she wanted it to be sacred to my future wife. I was blown away, and it was a journey down memory lane – *legacy* – seeing all of that old stuff again, much of which I had forgotten.

But she had not. I love that she passed down the legacy of memories to Janine, because I love to leave a legacy. My greatest legacy will be my sons, and the mark they leave on the world. And believe me, they will leave their mark. They are doing so even as we speak.

Every time a teacher compliments them to me. Every time a gymnastic teacher shares how well-behaved they are. Every time I see what an incredible craft Brennan has made. Every time Asher tells me he loves me. Every time they play well together and we hear them frolicking in the recesses of our home. Every time they demonstrate good manners and show kindness to others. Every time they do their chores, ahem, without complaining. Every time they express gratitude. Every time they demonstrate responsibility.

Every... single... time.

My boys are legacies in the making.

Let me tell you one last story. Sometimes legacies are left incorrectly, or irresponsibly. This happened with my boys and me.

I'm not only an author, but also a voiceover artist. I had just had my new voiceover booth constructed when we had our 880-square-foot shop built out beyond the concrete and framing that it had been for years. I had a custom voiceover booth constructed, along with an office, and converted the rest of the space into a rec room / workout area.

Well, along comes tiny little Asher, wandering into my voiceover booth with a pen. He decided to scribble all along the wall of my booth. The little guy was barely even two, but he made his mark. I got a bit upset. I didn't know which of them had done it, but I could only assume it was Asher based on the height of the scribble.

My love for, and my defense of, my new voiceover booth almost prevailed... until I remembered that Asher doesn't like getting into trouble. Remember the incident with the croc and my face? Well, he already knew he was in the wrong. That little guy confessed in tears with trembling lips. I scooped him up and told him it was okay, and that I love him. I smoothed away his tears and told him *thank you* for leaving a reminder in my booth that I have a beautiful son whom I love very much.

And then to Asher's amazement (and Brennan's pure delight), I had Brennan come in and make his *own* doodle on another wall of my voiceover booth. So now, I have a random scribble from Asher and a

Godzilla from Brennan hastily scrawled across two walls of my voiceover booth. But will a client ever see them? No, because I work in *checks notes* yep, *audio*. I was concerned about appearances, but thank God I realized that the only appearance I needed to be concerned about was what kind of legacy I was leaving for my boys after they defiled my voiceover booth: one of anger, or one of forgiveness?

Thank goodness I erred on the side of grace. Because now, I see it, I'm reminded of it, and I love it. I *love* that they scribbled on my walls. I love that they're with me in that studio, because I love *them* dearly, and I want them with me.

Legacy is all about making memories. And for me, *loving them well* is the best legacy I could ever leave…. It's the best memory they will ever retain.

DEAR BRENNAN AND ASHER:

May the legacy I leave always communicate dignity to you. May you only remember how overflowingly much I love you. May you yourself leave a legacy of love, because you came from love. Remember, he who has the most friends wins! And listen, because

someday listening will save your life! And be
grateful for what you do have, not angry about what
you don't! Those are legacies I wish to leave with
you, and may they equip you at need, but far and
away above that, may you always remember that
your daddy loved you with a beating heart, and that
heart was overflowing with pride at who you are and
who you've become.

Love,
Your Daddy

Chapter 9: When I Finally Understood

My old pastor, Lee Bennett, used to always preach on 'The Fatherheart of God.' He was, perhaps, in retrospect, overly preoccupied with The Prodigal Son. But who could blame him? The story rocks! He loved preaching on it, and at one point he had obtained a commission of Rembrandt's 'The Return of the Prodigal Son,⁹' which was huge, and framed prominently in the sanctuary of our old church.

He *loved* that story, and referenced it often. And for good reason. The father *loved* his son, and when he saw him returning after all those years living in debauchery and squandering his wealth, he was so overjoyed that he dropped everything and *ran* to him. He didn't want, judgmentally, angrily, for his son to return to him on his knees, demanding a renewed allegiance. No. He lowered himself and left everything behind to celebrate the return of that which was beloved… that which had been lost, and now was found.

Lee often preached on 'The Fatherheart of God' because it was so important to him for us to understand God's heart toward us: that He literally dropped everything and ran to us in the form of His Son, Jesus Christ.

I can't imagine losing either of my sons. It would disassemble me. It would ruin me, at least for a time. Pastor Lee also used to say, "having a child is like watching your heart walk around outside you." If someone *ever* took my heart…

I confess I never really understood how much of a role I had to play as a Father, or really understood God beyond a slightly Catholic sense of obedience = favor, disobedience = punishment. It's like, in some twisted way, I thought God might be Zeus, ready to hurl a lightning bolt at me for my messing up *yet again*. If that were true, I would whistle when I walked out of all the zillions of lightning holes burned straight through me. Thankfully, God is a bit more charitable than that.

There came a day when I was in the dining room of our home, and Asher, little 2-year-old Asher, came running to me and exclaimed "Up, up, up!" He approached me just as he usually did, but it was something in the way he did it this time that just caught me off guard. He raised his hands high, and he approached me with such abandon and trust, knowing that I would in no way reject him. He knew he was completely safe in approaching me, and that he had my favor and blessing.

For whatever reason, it shocked me and caught me completely off-guard. It taught me a valuable lesson that day. Asher knows his Daddy loves him. Asher knows that he's safe with me. Asher knows that I won't cast him away.

I saw God differently from that day forward. I know that He loves me. I know that I'm safe with him. I know that He won't cast me away.
In short, I saw the Fatherheart of God.

It also taught me that I can approach God that way, with my arms outstretched, wanting Him to pick me up, love me, carry me. That isn't the God I grew up believing in, and it isn't the God that many of us down here perceive. Far too many think of God as an angry, vindictive God, ready with those lightning bolts. Far too many choose not to trust Him because they think of Him as distant, removed, disinterested.

Nothing could be further from the truth. The Bible says the following about God:

Know therefore that the Lord your God is God; he is the faithful God, keeping his covenant of love to a thousand generations of those who love him and keep his commandments. – Deuteronomy 7:9

But you, Lord, are a compassionate and gracious God, slow to anger, abounding in love and faithfulness. – Psalms 86:15

Let the morning bring me word of your unfailing love, for I have put my trust in you. Show me the way I should go, for to you I entrust my life. – Psalm 143:8

For God so loved the world that he gave his one and only Son, that whoever believes in him shall not perish but have eternal life. – John 3:16

As the Father has loved me, so have I loved you. Now remain in my love. If you keep my commands, you will remain in my love, just as I have kept my Father's commands and remain in his love. – John 15:9-10

My command is this: Love each other as I have loved you. Greater love has no one than this: to lay down one's life for one's friends. – John 15:12-13

But God demonstrates his own love for us in this: While we were still sinners, Christ died for us. – Romans 5:8

Who shall separate us from the love of Christ? Shall trouble or hardship or persecution or famine or nakedness or danger or sword? As it is written: "For your sake we face death all day long; we are considered as sheep to be slaughtered." No, in all these things we are more than conquerors through him who loved us. For I am convinced that neither death nor life, neither angels nor demons, neither the present nor the future, nor any powers, neither height nor depth, nor anything else in all creation, will be able to separate us from the love of God that is in Christ Jesus our Lord. –Romans 8:35-39

But because of his great love for us, God, who is rich
in mercy, made us alive with Christ even when we
were dead in transgressions — it is by grace you have
been saved. –Ephesians 2:4-5

See what great love the Father has lavished on us,
that we should be called children of God! And that is
what we are! The reason the world does not know us
is that it did not know him. –1 John 3:1

We love because he first loved us. –1 John 4:19

And so we know and rely on the love God has for us.
God is love. Whoever lives in love lives in God, and
God in them. This is how love is made complete
among us so that we will have confidence on the day
of judgment: In this world we are like Jesus. There is
no fear in love. But perfect love drives out fear,
because fear has to do with punishment. The one who
fears is not made perfect in love. – 1 John 4:16-18

There are SO many more. The truth is that God loves
us unendingly. He loves us with a perfect love that
gives us what we need. Matthew 7:9-10 says "Which
of you, if your son asks for bread, will give him a

stone? Or if he asks for a fish, will give him a snake?"
Our Father knows what we need, and He knows we
need to be held and loved.

That simple, innocent act by Asher of trust and
drawing near to me communicated a great deal to me
about my worth as his Daddy, and about God's
worth as mine.

James 1:17 says 'Every good and perfect gift is from
above, coming down from the Father of the heavenly
lights, who does not change like shifting shadows.'[10]
I have always loved that verse because it
communicates stability. In a world where fathers
come and go, THE Father sticks around. He's
Daddy…. He's Abba…(Aramaic for 'Daddy') and He
does not change like shifting shadows. He's not
Denethor. He's not the decrepit steward of Gondor
who cursed his secondborn and wished that he had
died instead of his firstborn.

Now, I am not the kind of dad who would bark at my
kids if they came running out to the shop and caught
me in the middle of work, writing a story, talking to
someone in an interview, even recording a voiceover
with a client on the line. I have *seen* a contact of mine

do that while in a video chat with him, and it left an indelible impression on me: I vowed *never* to be that kind of father. My sons know they are always welcome to approach me during whatever I'm doing. (Except pooping, but we covered that earlier.) They are always welcome.

In fact, if I see them coming, I might just drop everything, and run out to them, so excited to see their return. Just like the Prodigal Son's father. Just like Abba.

Speaking of barking, if you're prone to outbursts and yelling at your kids, allow me to suggest something. Know your triggers. Perform that crucial self-assessment that helps you determine what sets you off, so that your kids don't come inadvertently wading into it and get punished for something they didn't do. And go even further than that! Give them permission to ask you a dreadfully spotlighting question: "Daddy, are you mad first about something *else?*" That question will invite a painful self-assessment where, if you're brutally honest, you'll admit that they don't deserve the extra anger you're heaping upon them.

Understand that they just want to be lifted up, held, and loved.

DEAR BRENNAN AND ASHER:

If I have ever made you feel unwelcome or undesired, shame on me. It is something I never should have done. I pray that you know that you are always welcome in every part of my life. Except when I'm pooping. I pray that you know that you can *always* approach me. Except when I'm pooping. I pray that you always understand, deep in your hearts, and I will always scoop you up, hold you tight, kiss you on your cheek and tell you that I love you.

Except when I'm pooping.

Love,
Daddy

Chapter 10: The Ring of Power

I am a sci-fi writer at heart. One could say I have a soft spot for science fiction. My books are mostly science fiction. Without a doubt, books such as the one you're reading – when I'm prompted to write them – take me well off the beaten path and away from sci-fi, entering into something real, tangible, vulnerable, honest, and human. Most of the time, though, science fiction is what I go for.

Then why on earth would I want to write kids picture books?!?!? I have two sons, so that's why. May I explain? Thank you, I will.

On occasion, Brennan battles feelings of shame. The act of doing something 'bad' makes him feel horrible about himself.

My wife and I are very careful to explain for him, "We may be disappointed in what you *did*; we are not disappointed in who you *are*." Brennan must realize that the two are drastically different. Guilt stems from wrongdoing. Shame revolves around identity.

After one such conversation with Brennan, I decided to read him a bedtime story. He dozed off while I shared the story with him purely from my imagination. The fact that he fell asleep either means that the story was either incredibly relaxing or incredibly boring.

However you slice it, in that tale, I imagined a young boy — 9 years old, naturally — who was tormented by monsters that never stopped telling him he was awful. The truth is that he did several things that some could call 'bad.' But he started to withdraw from people and isolate himself. To wallow in self-pity, constantly beset by the charges leveled against him by the aforementioned orcs, wargs, trolls, and ogres.

He would go out and kill dragons whenever his fits hit him. He found solace in that, as it restored his sense of being a decent human being. What he truly needed to defeat, though, were the demons dwelling *inside himself,* the ones that pointed bony accusing fingers in his direction, who blamed him not for his actions, but leveled epithets in his direction, attacking his very identity.

One day, however, a towering man wearing a ring paid him a visit. He was shrouded in a brilliant glow, making the man's identity a mystery to the youngster. The man extended a ring to the boy, which included a small button that the child could press. Pressing the ring's button would purge the negative energy around him, restoring his sense of self-worth and truth whenever he felt low.

Defeating the monsters became so easy for the child that he no longer needed his armor. The truth ring was at his disposal. I loved the story I told him so much that I eventually went on to publish my first children's book. Subsequently, *The Ring of Truth* and *The Sword of Joy* were released in 2024 (followed shortly thereafter by *The Book of Power,* to make it a trilogy).

When I presented *The Ring of Truth* to Brennan, he loved it. But so did Asher, who was five years old at the time. Why I didn't see Asher's next remark coming, I have no idea. It caught me off guard. Asher exclaimed, "That's great, Daddy, where's *mine?*" Ha! Well, time to write a new book, I guess. Because of that, that's why I decided to write *The Sword of Joy,* and then the final installment. Now, each son has his own story.

All three fall under *The Christian Kids Values, Identity and Affirmation Picture Book Series.*[11]

The reason I'm getting into this is because I wanted to teach my son a lesson about the importance of self-esteem, something I experienced firsthand as a child. After John the Baptist baptized Jesus in the Jordan, God the Father spoke precisely those words to Him. "You are my beloved son, in whom I am well pleased." he declared.

I adore that expression, and I use it often, as you'll see clearly in this book.

"Dear Brennan, you are my beloved son, in whom I am well pleased," I tell him. "Nothing you could ever do could ever take away my love for you; that is the meaning of the phrase. Your position with me is secure, and nothing you do could change that. You would remain in my good graces regardless of what you did. To put it simply, I LOVE YOU."

Asher gets the same phrase directed at him often. They are utterly loved, and they know it. And in that, there is no shame. There is no condemnation. They are my beloved sons, in whom I am well pleased.

DEAR BRENNAN AND ASHER:

You *are* my beloved sons, in whom I am *well* pleased. Are you perfect? No. Far from it, just like me. It's like one of your Daddy's favorite T-Shirts that says, 'Am I perfect? No. But am I trying to be a better person? Also no.'

You and I are just trying to do the very best we can, and I love you for trying, for improving, for learning, for growing, for offering yourself to the world as honestly and authentically as possible, with all of your wins, your losses, your credits, your debits, your strengths, your flaws, your perfections as well as your imperfections, and everything that makes you *you.* In all of it, I am *well pleased* with you. I mean it.

I am so proud of you, I adore you, and I am *so* blessed that you are mine.

Love,
Daddy

Chapter 11: Papa

Any man can be a father, but my father is my Dad.

Yes, he's turning eighty next year, but you wouldn't know it. Jerry is a loving soul, gracious in words, giving in deed, love in action and spiritual with power. He is the Dad I needed right when I needed him.

I have such fond memories of growing up with my Dad. Playing 'Happy Dog Mad Dog' where he, on his hands and knees, would approach me and my brothers while panting happily like a friendly dog. We would pet him with great trepidation knowing that at any minute, without warning, he would suddenly explode into "MAD DOG RAWWWRRR!!!" and we would all flee shrieking into the distance. I *love* that playful memory of him.

All the times playing catch with him. My dad was an athlete in high school before being scouted by the Pittsburgh Pirates and then being drafted into Vietnam. He pitched a no-hitter in high school! He taught me how to throw correctly, how to bat correctly, and all those times where we would go play catch, where he would bat the ball way out into the outfield and would cheer me on like nobody's business when I chased down flyballs. I've never had someone root me on so vociferously or with such joy.

Having him lightly tickle the undersides of my feet when I was a boy, sending me to sleep.

The one time he got so angry with me. I can't remember what I did; it was probably mouthing off or something like that, I don't remember... but who cares: the important point is that he was livid over some misbehavior, and I fled from him into the kitchen. On my way in, I accidentally knocked loose a small chalkboard on the wall. It swung perilously on its remaining top nail, hitting dad squarely in the face on his way in, which made him even more mad. I watched his reaction with terror, watched him turn even a darker shade of red, yell, and come at me with even more ferocity. I cringed, recoiling into myself…

…and he never once hit me. He never once laid a hand on me.

When he got saved, renouncing his old life and being made into a new person through salvation in Christ. Having him join me on this side of salvation, knowing his eternity was now secure.

When I went through a tremendously painful and life-altering ordeal in 2000, and he stepped up, becoming the Dad I needed, the friend I craved, the support I could lean on, the prayer warrior I knew I could depend on.

Jerry isn't just my father; he's my *Dad.* I talked earlier about how anyone can become a biological father in the chapter, 'Just Any Dad.' It takes a special kind of soul, a bold soul, a determined and honorable soul, to step up and be a Dad to their sons. My Dad was there for me, and he still is, in every way.

He dotes on my children. He honors and cherishes my wife. He adores our family. He spends time with us. He generously lavishes his love and gifts on us. He actively sows into our lives. He calls regularly. He is always praying for us. Remember your best tool in your bag of tricks?

Jerry's got that one down pat.

When I was in music, I once wrote a song for my Dad, and I'd like to share it here. It's a song that attests to my Dad being exactly who I needed, and it was with utter gratitude that I presented it to him on an album I produced back in 2010.

Here are the lyrics:

Society tells us what we're worth, but formed from the earth, how much can there be?
To bring home the bread and bacon too, the chosen few, what more do we need?
But something deep in us satisfies, squashes the lies of history
The hardened resolve of mankind, this like mind can set us free

The truth from above, when push comes to shove, is that we all need an archetype

A perfect ideal, example surreal,
a father figure to end the hype

Papa you are the man, you help me stand,
you're there when love is in demand
You lift me up, you fill my cup,
you showed me how to be a man
And I can't believe God gave you to me, you love
lavishly
Papa I'm your biggest fan - you're my kind of man

Embodiment of such certainty, reality, you pave the way
A radiance beaming in dark times,
filling my mind, you light my day
A tree that bends beneath its load,
yet remains bold, your roots are strong
A weary pilgrim travelling,
still you sing courageous song

When I wanna hide, roll over and die,
that's when I espy your flags unfurled
And I rise again, determined to win,
and run to the end, my arms awhirl

Papa you are the man, you help me stand,
you're there when love is in demand
You lift me up, you fill my cup,

you showed me how to be a man
And I can't believe God gave you to me, you love
lavishly
Papa I'm your biggest fan - you're my kind of man

I am my Dad's biggest fan. I'm so proud of the man
he's become, because it's the man I want to become.
I'm so in awe of his unflappable spirit, because it's
the kind of spirit I want. *The joy of the Lord is his*
strength, like Nehemiah 8:10 says.

I love him unfailingly. My Dad has brought God
closer to me, and be closer to God, by showing me
what a loving father is truly like. I have a loving
father, and The Loving Father. As with a mirror,
looking back on what I described with Asher in
'When I Finally Understood,' I understood God
better, and how He sees me. With my own father,
I'm more like Asher: I understand God better, and
how I see Him.

I'm beyond grateful for the example my dad
continues to set for me. Like I said, we'll celebrate his
80th birthday next year, but the guy is practically 40
with his zest for life, his unflappable joy, and his

longing to see people saved and show the love of Jesus to them.

Most of all, I'm just darned proud of him, and I want to be more like him every single day.

DEAR DAD:

Papa, you are the man. You're my kind of man. I love you with all my heart, and I thank you for being the kind of Dad I needed, when I needed him. If I could be a tenth of the man that you are, I'd be a happy camper.

I love you, Pops. Thank you for being Jesus with skin on for me. I'm a better Daddy because I had the best Dad.

Thank you for making me feel like I was your whole Earth.

Love,
Your Son

Chapter 12: You Are My Whole Earth

"Yes," said Gandalf, "I never told him, but its worth was greater than the value of the whole Shire and everything in it."

Those words were spoken by the wizard to Gimli while fumbling about in the dark of Moria. The Fellowship were struggling to make it through to the other side of the mountain, and making small talk amongst themselves. In that conversation, Gandalf mentioned to Gimli – and by extension the rest of the Fellowship – that Thorin Oakenshield had once given Bilbo a coat of mithril mail armor. It was among the many treasures that Bilbo returned to the Shire with.

Unbeknownst to Bilbo, the value of that coat was greater than the entire province that the hobbits – and the surrounding folk for miles – lived in. *As well as everything in it.*

I got to thinking, how often do we give kingly gifts? What kingly gift can I give to my two princes?

My sons, Brennan and Asher, are my princes, heirs to my and my queen's kingdom. Wouldn't I give them anything? They are worth more than everything I see.

They are my whole Earth and everything in it.

The Earth is 12,756 kilometers across the equator. It's a planet teeming with all kinds of life and possibility. It has 5.49 quadrillion square feet over 179 million square surface miles. It is vast, some of it is uncharted, it is beautiful, glorious, expansive, and wonderful. Within the Earth's crust, silicates such as Feldspar and Quartz predominate, while in the interior, Bridgmanite, a magnesium iron silicate, constitutes 40% of the total volume and is the most prevalent mineral by volume. There are more than 5,000 known varieties of minerals on the planet. The metals iron, gold, and silver are plentiful. Silicon, aluminum, and calcium, among other valuable metals, are plentiful. Plus, there's oxygen, the life-giving gas.

Earth is *amazing*. And my sons mean more to me than this entire planet and everything in it.

Bilbo couldn't have known that he was walking around with the price of the Shire under his shirt. And neither could Frodo, once Bilbo had bequeathed it to him in Rivendell. They both knew it was valuable, yes, but *how* valuable was unclear to them. Certainly, to have something that you wear appraised for more than the gross national product... more than the entire *worth* of a small country... would blow your mind.

So then the question becomes, how exactly do I demonstrate this value to my sons?

Easy.

- Paying attention to them.
- Cheering them on.
- Sacrificing for them.
- Spending quality time with them.

- Not settling for a "fine" when I ask how their day was. Probing further.
- Showing them that they are the center of my very universe.
- Reveling in their every invention.
- Celebrating their every milestone.
- Taking pictures of them.
- Being silly with them.
- Being serious with them.
- Being honest with them.
- Being firm with them.
- Being loose with them.
- Being disciplined with them.
- Assuring them that they can talk to us about *anything*.
- Empowering them to live independently.

That daily journal I mentioned earlier? It is something I can't wait to give to both of my sons. In that journal are moments of our lives, snapshots of who they were at the time, what we all were going through, what life was like, and everything else that goes into raising a family. But at the core of it, it speaks to a Daddy whose sons were important enough to be on his mind constantly. I'm an author, and I write all the time. I weep over characters that don't exist, in places that don't exist, during circumstances that don't exist. (Don't judge me.) But my sons are real, in real times, in real places, and their lives are far from fiction; they are the ultimate reality, and I get to sow into that in ways I never will for a character in a book. They are my very pride and joy, my heart and soul.

I had no intention of making it to 12 chapters in this book, but it's fitting. My kids were born on the 12th of the month, we were married in '12, we were engaged on the June 12th, we're Seahawks fans (12's)... it's fate, I guess.

Just like in Iron Man, when Tony Stark's daughter tells her daddy, "I love you 3,000," this is the same. To that little girl, 3,000 is an incomprehensibly *massive* number, unimaginable, unattainable, unmatched in scale. Well, I love my kids 3,000. (But, truthfully, it's more like 3 quadrillion x pi to the power of infinity + one.) Many of these expressions exist over the whole world.

- "I love you to pieces."
- "You're the cheese to my macaroni."

- "You've stolen a pizza my heart."
- "Yoda one for me."
- "I'm stuck on you like glue."
- "You are my sunshine."
- "You complete me."
- "I love you to the moon and back."

And, the best one… "You are my whole Earth." I *so* love my sons. They are my life's greatest achievement, my greatest honor, my greatest responsibility, and my greatest passion. I get to watch them grow, day by day. I am bestowed with the rich honor of being by their side every day of their little lives, and hopefully a ton of their days as young adults and adults. I am *so* proud of them.

We tell our boys that they can talk to us about absolutely anything. No shame. No embarrassment. We'll never make them feel silly for asking. Brennan is getting to that age where he's starting to ask more in depth questions about anatomy and sex. I'm so proud that he feels comfortable enough to be able to come to me with his questions. I didn't have that same access or comfort with my own parents. As a result, I had to figure out a lot of things of that nature for myself. We want our boys to know that we are safe, and that there is no shame. Remember *The Ring of Truth*? Shame is a *powerful* enemy of youth; kids who walk around wrapped in shame are a hair's breadth away from self-destruction, even suicide. Satan *loves* to wrap up kids in shame, paralyzing them, emasculating them from efficiency, effectiveness, valor, worth, promise, destiny. It's our job to cut through those snares and be their safe harbor.

We have a thing in our home where I ask the boys how much I love them. They both know what to do. They will outstretch their arms as horrendously far as they possibly can, lower their voice into a booming monstrosity of noise, and exclaim, slowly, dropped in pitch to emphasize the magnanimity of it, *"Thiiiiiiiiiiiiiiiiiiis muuuuuuuccccchhhhh....."*

Because I do. I love them, ahem, **stretches out arms, lowers voice* thiiiiiiiiiiiiiiiiiiiiiiis muuuuuuuuuuuuuuuch.* It's not hard to understand why, really, if you think about it. It's because they are my whole Earth, and everything in it.

I love you 3 quadrillion x pi to the power of infinity + one, Brennan and Asher. Always and forever.

Love,

Your Daddy

PS, dear reader, if you're a daddy, may you love someone as fully too. May you be present and involved. May you be not a Father, but a Daddy.

Love,

Aaron Ryan

Afterword

Sometimes, right smack dab in the middle of another book I'm writing, I'll get an idea that will veer me off course, require me to press the pause button, and engage a totally new line of thought that had no branches to, origin in, or connection with what I was writing at the time. I'm flippant and impulsive like that, but I need to chase whatever thought is beckoning to me from my consciousness or spirit.

This book is the byproduct of one of those lines of thought.

I was working on the second book in my post-apocalyptic *Talisman* series when *You are my whole Earth* came calling.

And, like a good bloodhound, I immediately gave chase and followed the breadcrumbs. Each book is a bone, each writing process is a hunt, and I am a dog on the trail. I'm a fiction writer, but if I get a germ of an idea for a nonfiction *-or other kind of-* book, I've got to pause, reverse course, and explore that other path fully, seeing where it leads.

I love my sons, and I want to leave them a world that is full of rich possibilities, adventure, thrills, highs, accomplishments, peaks, and great success in whatever they do. *Success is a process,* as Richie Norton said, *not an event.*[12] Their whole life is a process of success. I pray their journey takes them to the highest peaks, and, yes, even the lowest dungeons, so that they can see how the other half lives; find what works for them; realize how good they truly have it, and become successful through all of that learning.

With the daily journal that I keep for both boys, I've wanted to leave them both a legacy that speaks to the fact that I was always thinking about them. Always considering their futures, blessing them, praying for them, etc.. Recording our most important memories from the day… week… month… year. At this writing, it's the end of 2025, and Brennan is 9. Asher is 6. I plan on giving this journal to them when they reach 18. It is, as of this writing, Arial font 9, two columns on each page, 291 pages.

Now, it will be a long time before I give them this journal, but I live for the day when I can do so, communicating to them that they are my whole Earth. Their value is far beyond this tiny orb in space, and everything on it. I want them to know how utterly precious they are to me... how unadulteratedly sacred they are... how invaluable their souls are, and how rich the bounty of their lives I pray will be. They are miracles, and nothing short, and they have *so* blessed me. So, I choose to bless them back and tell them how much I love them, how much I *have* loved them, how much I will *always* love them, and how, as God said to His Son Jesus, "You are my beloved son, in whom I am well pleased." That is a common refrain running through the daily journal I record for them, and it is mentioned countless times both therein and herein, because it's utterly true.

They are my whole Earth.

I pray this book serves a great purpose in motivating you to be a better Daddy or parent; that it reaches the hearts of fathers and mothers everywhere to constantly extend their love to their children, underscoring how important our children are; how much destiny they have; what profound belief we have in them.

Brennan, Asher, you are my beloved sons, in whom I am well pleased. You are my whole Earth.

Sincerely,

Aaron Ryan
aka 'Daddy'

Resources

Positive Parenting Solutions[13]

The Daily Dad by Ryan Holiday[14]

The Intentional Father by Jon Tyson[15]

Wild at Heart by John Eldredge[16]

Healing the Masculine Soul by Gordon Dalbey[17]

Healing for the Father Wound by H. Norman Wright[18]

About the Author

Award-winning and bestselling author, speaker,
panelist, workshop presenter and voice actor Aaron
Ryan lives in Washington with his wife and two sons,

along with Macy the dog, Winston the cat, and the finches Inky, Pinky, Blinky & Clyde.

He is the prolific author of the bestselling *Dissonance* 6-book alien invasion saga, the Christian dystopian fiction trilogy *The End*, the *Talisman* trilogy, the sci-fi thrillers *Forecast, The Slide,* and *The Phoenix Experiment*, the nonfiction books *God Is Not Santa, You Are My Whole Earth, You're Going Straight To Helen (In A Handbasket)* and *Aaron Ryan presents "A Lyrical Empirical Satirical Miracle,"* the children's picture books *The Ring of Truth, The Sword of Joy* and *The Book of Power*, the business reference books *How to Successfully Self-Publish & Promote Your Self-Published Book* and *The Superhero Anomaly*, 6 business books on voiceovers penned under his former stage name (Joshua Alexander), as well as a previous fictional novel, *The Omega Room*.

When he was in second grade, he was tasked with writing a creative assignment: a fictional book. And thus, *The Electric Boy* was born: a simple novella full of intrigue, fantasy, and 7-year-old wits that electrified Aaron's desire to write. From that point forward, Aaron evolved into a creative soul that desired to create.

He enjoys the arts, media, music, performing, poetry, and being a daddy. In his lifetime he has been an author, voiceover artist, wedding videographer, stage performer, musician, producer, rock/pop artist, executive assistant, service manager, paperboy, CSR, poet, tech support, worship leader, and more. The diversity of his life experiences gives him a unique approach to business, life, ministry, faith, and entertainment.

Aaron's favorite author by far is J.R.R. Tolkien, but he also enjoys Suzanne Collins, James S.A. Corey, Michael Crichton, Marie Lu, Madeleine L'Engle, John Grisham, Tom Clancy, Tim Lebbon, Christopher Golden, C.S. Lewis, Stephen King and Dave Barry.

Aaron has always had a passion for storytelling. Visit his website at https://www.authoraaronryan.com, join his exclusive and private Facebook group at https://authoraaronryangroup.com, or check out his store at https://authoraaronryanstore.com.

If you liked this or any of Aaron's books, please visit the Amazon and Goodreads pages for the specific book(s) and leave a positive review. Once it shows up, please email the screenshot of it to me@authoraaronryan.com for a discount on your next book purchase from him! Thank you so much. Reviews really do help a ton!

Visit Aaron's website and sign up at the Blog:

Subscribe to Author Aaron Ryan

Follow Aaron and connect on Social Media:

Connect with Aaron

Feel free to check out the following links for further information on Aaron:

Subscribe to Aaron's blog for free giveaways, news and new releases at authoraaronryan.com/blog

Join the Author Aaron Ryan Facebook community at facebook.com/groups/authoraaronryan

Subscribe to Aaron's YouTube channel at youtube.com/@authoraaronryan

Visit Aaron's social media links to connect with him at dot.cards/authoraaronryan

Visit Aaron's website at authoraaronryan.com

Follow Aaron on IMDb at imdb.me/authoraaronryan

Also by the Author

As Aaron Ryan:

1. *Dissonance Volume I: Reality*
2. *Dissonance Volume II: Reckoning*
3. *Dissonance Volume III: Renegade*
4. *Dissonance Volume IV: Relentless*
5. *Dissonance Volume Zero: Revelation*
6. *Dissonance Volume Up: Rising*
7. *The Complete Dissonance Alien Invasion Saga*
8. *THE END: Alpha*
9. *THE END: Omicron*
10. *THE END: Omega*
11. *The Complete THE END Christian Dystopian Saga*
12. *Forecast*
13. *The Slide*
14. *The Phoenix Experiment*
15. *Thrillerumvirate*
16. *Talisman: Subterfuge*
17. *Talisman: Nexus*
18. *Talisman: Halcyon*
19. *The Complete Talisman Series*
20. *The Ring of Truth*
21. *The Sword of Joy*

22. *The Book of Power*
23. *The Christian Kids Values, Identity & Affirmation Series*
24. *God Is Not Santa*
25. *You are my whole Earth: A Daddy's Love For His Sons*
26. *You're Going Straight To Helen (In A Handbasket)*
27. *A Lyrical Empirical Satirical Miracle*
28. *Examining The Lord of the Rings: An independent critique by Aaron Ryan*
29. *The Superhero Anomaly*
30. *How to Successfully Self-Publish & Promote Your Independent Book: A Self-Publishing & Business Marketing Guide For The Independent Author*
31. *Reflections: A Compilation of Journals and Poetry*
32. *The Omega Room (abandoned in the early 90's)*
33. *Autobiography (no longer available)*
34. *Glimmerings – works of poetry*

As his former stage name, Josh Alexander:

35. *Voiceovers: A Super Business, A Super Life*
36. *Voiceovers: A Super Fun Pursuit*
37. *Voiceovers: A Super Responsibility*
38. *Running a Successful Voiceover Business*
39. *How do I get started in Voiceovers?*
40. *Five T's to Triumph: The Secrets to Getting Cast in Voiceovers*

Bibliography

[1] https://open.spotify.com/track/6OE3JHIMfAfgjjfosZ2iUu
[2] https://en.wikipedia.org/wiki/Collect_call
[3] https://www.rd.com/list/heartwarming-stories-of-dads-going-above-and-beyond/
[4] https://www.imdb.com/title/tt0084516/characters/nm0748289/
[5] https://www.kiro7.com/news/local/majority-washington-schools-will-have-cell-phone-policy-this-fall/QDWFZNJA6NBZRBUGJXDEAQE3X4/
[6] https://www.amazon.com/dp/194820956X?ref_=ppx_hzsearch_conn_dt_b_fed_asin_title_4
[7] *Morte d'Arthur* by Alfred Lord Tennyson
[8] https://www.cnn.com/2015/08/11/asia/gallery/china-father-son-same-picture-three-decades
[9] https://bigcanvasartprints.com/products/the-return-of-the-prodigal-son-1669-by-rembrandt
[10] https://www.biblegateway.com/passage/?search=James%201%3A17&version=NIV
[11] https://www.christianpicturebook.com
[12] https://quotefancy.com/quote/3802911/Richie-Norton-Success-is-a-process-not-an-event
[13] Positiveparentingsolutions.com
[14] https://www.amazon.com/Daily-Dad-Meditations-Parenting-Raising/dp/0593539052
[15] https://www.audible.com/pd/The-Intentional-Father-Audiobook/B09FCPMJKH?source_code=AUDORWS0718179KY7
[16] https://en.wikipedia.org/wiki/Wild_at_Heart_(Eldredge_book)
[17] https://www.amazon.com/Healing-Masculine-Soul-Restoration-Manhood/dp/0849944384/
[18] https://www.amazon.com/Healing-Father-Wound-Christian-Time-Tested/dp/0764205358

www.ingramcontent.com/pod-product-compliance
Lightning Source LLC
Chambersburg PA
CBHW071747120626
46550CB00002B/700